from the Archives

OF THE UNIVERSE CATHOLIC WEEKLY

from the Archives

OF THE UNIVERSE CATHOLIC WEEKLY

A selection of images from the popular magazine series

by Joseph Kelly

THE UNIVERSE CATHOLIC WEEKLY

This edition first published in 2010 by
The Universe Media Group Limited

ISBN 9-781904-657637

Designed by The Universe Media Group Ltd
Printed in the UK by Antony Rowe Limited, Bumper's Farm, Chippenham, Wiltshire SN14 6LH

For enquiries contact: The Universe Media Group Ltd, 4th Floor Landmark House, Station Road, Cheadle Hulme, Cheshire SK8 7JH. Tel: 0161 488 1760

Website: www.totalcatholic.com

Editor: Joseph Kelly
Research and proofing : Michael Winterbottom and Lynda Walker
Design and production: Brendan Gilligan
Marketing: Andrea Black
Online Sales: Chris Morley

Archive project reveals unique history of Catholic Faith

W hen *The Universe Catholic weekly* left London for its present home in Manchester, its extensive picture library came with it. Occupying an annex to the newsroom, it rapidly fell into disuse with the advent of the electronic media age and the digital camera. With the passage of time events, names and subject matters also became obscure and forgotten, and the countless stored images became increasingly dated and unusable in our modern publications.

Founded in 1860, *The Universe* spent most of its life in and around London's Fleet Street, where it enjoyed unique and privileged access to Catholic events and personalities, at a time when the wider media world regarded Catholicism with suspicion and considerable misunderstanding. Thus *The Universe* rapidly became both a significant Catholic news agency, and an important picture library for the rest of Fleet Street.

With significantly increasing sales - 9,000 in 1919 to 300,000 in 1959 - *The Universe* found itself at the cutting edge of the newspaper industry. At this time it was the longest web offset print run in the world, and had already been one of the first UK newspapers to use photographs, and to introduce colour images. Employing the services of some of the most respected photographers of the day - including the legendary Bert Hardy of *Picture Post fame* - *The Universe* picture archive from the first half of the 20th century is not only a remarkably high quality and informative chronicle of our Catholic community, but is a a social and cultural record of considerable importance.

Despite working every day only yards away from this amazing resource, it was only in 2002 that I began to explore the dusty cabinets and crumbling wallets, in search of reference material for a Catholic history book that I am working on. At first the collection was difficult to appreciate, as many pictures had been filed using references and names that were undoubtedly very obvious to all and sundry at the time, but that meant little or nothing to me. But what astounded me, time and again, was the sheer quality of images - the skill in composition, the clarity of the pictures, and the wealth of social and cultural information that the many prints contained.

Incredibly, the *Universe*'s vast collection of negatives had been dumped during the move to Manchester, so it became apparent that I was looking at a truly unique piece of Catholic history which, if lost, could never be recovered.

At first I devoted what little spare time I had to cataloguing and preserving the most significant images, but more recently we have begun to approach the task in a more organised fashion and, to date, we have more than 10,000 images stored and catalogued electronically, as well as making a considerable investment in microfiching the many supporting documents, and issues of *The Universe* going back to 1860. It's a massive task, and I anticipate that the project may still take a further five years to complete, but the result will be a unique and vitally significant record of the Catholic community in the 150 years since the Restoration.

To help finance this ongoing project we have published an annual magazine, *From the Archives*, featuring some of the best of the images. The magazine can be found in Catholic parishes across the UK and Ireland, and is also available for digital download at our website *www.totalcatholic.com,* where you will also find Irish, Scotish and American editions of the magazine.

Many subscibers have been asking if we could produce a hardbound edition of *From the Archives*, so here it is. I do hope you enjoy this selection, which offers a succinct and intriguing snapshot of so many aspects of Catholic Life across the 20th century.

Joseph Kelly

CEO
The Universe Media Group Limited

Editor:
The Universe
Who's Who in Catholic Life
From the Archives
Church Building & Heritage Review

Catholic newspaper that set the standard

To put the launch of *The Universe* Catholic weekly into the context of Church history, it was just two years after the apparitions of Our Lady at Lourdes, and six years after Pope Pius IX defined the dogma of the Immaculate Conception, which stated that Our Lady was conceived without stain of Original Sin, that the first *Universe* appeared.

Only 31 years earlier, Catholics had received recognition with passing of the Catholic Emancipation Act and, in 1847, four new Catholic districts were created - Eastern, Central, Welsh and Lancashire.

But it was not until 1850-51 that the first bishops were appointed with Cardinal Nicholas Wiseman as the head of the Church in England and Wales.

Archibald Dunn was the first Editor and SVP member, Denis Lane, the printer. The first copies of *The Universe* were published on Saturday, December 8, 1860 - at a cover price of one penny - from 43 Lamb's Conduit Street, London WC.

The front page announced that "a cheap Catholic newspaper is required - if only to stay the circulation of anti-Catholic weekly newspapers among Catholic families resident in London".

"We are not large capitalists," announced the editorial, "but practical workers". Annual subscription cost 4s 4d and advertisements 6d for three lines, with each additional line costing 2d. The paper declared on its front page, under the heading 'Address', that it would "uphold the dignity and independence of the Church both at home and abroad" and "shall be deaf to no cry of human suffering

from whatever quarter it may come" and would be on the side of "the weak and the oppressed in days of trouble".

By selling the paper for just one penny a copy, *The Universe* said it hoped to be a weekly paper "within the reach of all classes". *The Tablet*, by comparison, cost 6d.

The *Universe*'s front page stories were concerned with elections in Naples and allegations of corruption, an announcement that the "Holy Father's treasury is now well nigh exhausted, and Baron Rothschild announces publicly that the interest on the Papal loan which was due on the 1st inst., has not been remitted by the 3rd.

Meanwhile, however, the 'St Peter's Pence' is beginning to flow in pretty rapidly; £65,000 has been received from

America. We trust that the proceeds from our 'St Peter's Pence' Association in England may prove as large".

Inside, articles included a 'Dr Cullen on mixed marriages", an extract from a letter of the Archbishop of Tuam to Lord Palmerston regarding people of Party being banished from their homes, police news from London courts and, on the back page, a feature on Westminster Abbey.

In fact, in its eight pages of pure type, *The Universe*, as today, managed to cover a cross section of events both at home and abroad, of interest to Catholics.

Fifty years later – Friday December 9 1910 – *The Universe* had incorporated *Catholic Weekly* into its title, had increased its number of pages to 20 and carried advertisements for prayer books, Christmas cards, crib sets and missals and suggested presents for priests on its front page. Letters to the Editor column were concerned with abolition of capital punishment, a landslip at St Aloysius School, Highgate, and hymns in honour of the Immaculate Conception.

As with *The Universe* of today, it contained bishops' engagements, and in 'Outlook' an article anticipating the beginning of the second decade of the 20th century, some very prophetic statements were made concerning unrest in the world, which four years later was to manifest itself in the outbreak of the First World War.

By 1910, *The Universe* was giving news from all over the country, not just from London. Parliamentary elections were in progress and the paper ran a list of Catholic candidates for 17 constituencies.

But polling did not take place in the various places on the same day. Chichester and Howdenshire were voting on the 9th December, but Chepstow not until the following Tuesday and Buckrose, Friday, a week later.

For the 'golden jubilee' edition there was a blessing from the Pope and tributes from the Archbishop of Westminster and the English Catholic bishops.

The first editor, Archibald J Dunn, reminiscing on the beginnings, said that internationally the Church had suffered in 1860 with the seizing of Church property in Italy by Mazzini who had preached for the unification of Italy. Rome had been occupied by the revolutionary mob and the Press in England had a field day "for the fall of Rome meant to them the fall of the Roman Catholic faith".

"The daily papers teemed with falsehoods concerning the Pope, the bishops and clergy of Italy and to contradiction of these was allowed to appear in *The Times* or other journals."

Cardinal Wiseman agreed to forming a committee to set up a Catholic paper to defend Catholic interests at home and abroad. The first committee were all members of the St Vincent de Paul Society.

Later, Mr Dunn recalls St Peter's Pence Association was set up in the Universe offices, as well as the SVP's Home for Destitute Catholic Boys.

By 1910 the paper had started to produce photographs, mainly portraits of people mentioned in stories. It had by then also changed its address to 1 Racquet Court, Fleet Street, London EC.

Another 50 years on and the date is Thursday, the 8th December, 1960, and *The Universe* "The Catholic Family Newspaper" celebrated its centenary with a special front colour issue, carrying portraits of two Popes, Pope Pius IX (1860) and the much-loved Pope John XXIII, a flashback to the first front page and a fine drawing of St Peter's, Rome.

The cover price had increased to 4d and *The Universe*'s address was now Universe House, 21 Fleet Street. Bishop Beck of Salford, the bishops' spokesman on education, examined the growth of the Catholic Church in England since 1860 and concluded Catholics per cent of population had increased from four per cent in 1860, to seven per cent in 1960. Today the figure

is nearly eight per cent or 4,031,029 Catholics out of a population of 46,088,831.

On the back page of the 32 page edition, Dr Fisher, the Archbishop of Canterbury, returning from a visit to see the Pope, announced to readers: "I did not have to create an attitude of friendship, I walked straight into it."

To move on another 25 years, to Friday, the 6th December, 1985, and *The Universe* celebrated its 125th anniversary. The front page splash story in that edition was a call for a new catechism. And an extraordinary synod in Rome the proposal was made by French, German and Italian language groups. Another study group, headed by Cardinal Hume, proposed a 10-year programme of evangelism to run until the end of the century.

The price per copy had risen to 30p and the address was 33-39 Bowling Green Lane, London. Other stories to make the news were Lambeth Borough Council's refusal to allow the Knights of St Columba to erect a crib on Streatham Common and Archbishop Worlock's thoughts on the Church of England's report on inner cities. Letters to the editor were concerned with pro-life issues and the Warnock committee, Sunday trading and the erosion of vocations.

On the 7th October 1990 we produced our first issue from Manchester. It was a momentous occasion, not only in moving from Bowling Green Lane to Oxford Street, Manchester, but also in switching from contract typesetters to desktop publishing using Apple Macintosh computers.

Since then modern technology has moved on at a furious pace, and *The*

Universe has expanded from a single newspaper company into a modern, sophisticated publishing house with more than 15 titles in its portfolio, including *The Catholic Times*, *Catholic Life*, *The Catholic Companion*, *The Who's Who in Catholic Life*, the *English Catholic Directory*, *Church Building & Heritage Review*, as well as a whole range of special Catholic publications designed, produced and distributed for organisations such as the National Conference of Priests, the Catholic Women's League, the Union of Catholic Mothers and the Catenians.

In addition, our online brand – **www.totalcatholic.com** - offers a comprehensive Catholic shop, and the facility to download our publications from anywhere in the world.

150 years after the first issue rolled off the presses, *The Universe* remains true to its mission of being "a light to guide the world, and a mirror to reflect it", keeping Catholics informed about their faith, and bringing them ever closer to God.

Archbishop Peter Emanuel Amigo of Southwark pictured at Bromley in June 1939 with some of the Sisters of the Holy Trinity whose convent he blessed and opened. Peter Amigo was born in Gibraltar in 1864. He studied at St Edmund's, Ware, and St. Thomas's, Hammersmith, and was ordained priest in 1888. He was professor at St. Edmund's from September 1888, to July 1892, and was assistant priest at Hammersmith from September 1892, to June 1896. He then went to St. Mary's and St. Michael's, Commercial Road, East London, first as assistant priest, then as rector until April 1901, when he was then appointed rector of the mission at Walworth. He was consecrated Bishop of Southwark on the 25th March 1904. Having received the personal title of Archbishop on the 18th December 1937, he remained in control of the diocese until his death on the 1st October 1949.

One of London's biggest ARP posts during the Second World War was this convent in London, which couldn't be identified for security reasons. The photographer for *The Universe* was given special access and took this study of stretcher parties on exercise in the convent garden, watched by two of the nuns who had taken a break from preparing meals for the men in October 1939.

Pilgrims queue to receive Communion during the 1985 Middlesbrough Annual Diocesan pilgrimage to the shrine of Our Lady of Mount Grace, Ostmotherly, North Yorkshire. Mount Grace Priory, Ostmotherley, is one of only nine Carthusian priories founded in this country and is the best preserved. The 16th century Chapel of Our Lady of Mount Grace lies on a hill some 30 minutes walk above the priory. In 1665, the Franciscans took up residence and for a time young friars received their training in Osmotherley. The Franciscans ministered to the pilgrims, remaining there until 1832. The ruined chapel was bought in 1942 by the Roman Catholic diocese of Middlesbrough and by 1959 was restored. In 1969 the Franciscans returned and the buildings were expanded to cater for more pilgrims. Later, the monks of Ampleforth Abbey took their place. It is also famous as the burial place of St. Margaret Clitherow of York. Margaret was literally crushed to death by having heavy stones placed on her chest because she would not admit to having sheltered Catholic priests. She died on Lady Day 1586 and it is believed that they carried her body for burial to Osmotherley, to the Chapel of Our Lady of Mount Grace.

erbert **Alfred Vaughan** (April 15, 1832 – June 19, 1903) was born at Gloucester, the eldest son of Lieutenant-Colonel John Francis Vaughan, head of an old recusant family, the Vaughans of Courtfield, Herefordshire. His mother, a convert, Eliza Rolls from The Hendre, Monmouthshire, was intensely religious; and all five of the Vaughan family's daughters became nuns, while six of the eight sons took Holy Orders, becoming priests, with three of them being chosen as bishops.

Herbert spent six years at Stonyhurst College, and was then sent to study with the Benedictines at Downside Abbey, near Bath, and subsequently at the Jesuit school of Brugelette, Belgium, which was afterwards relocated to Paris.

In 1851 he went to Rome and, after a period of study at the Academia Dei Nobili Ecclesiastiae, where he became a friend and disciple of Henry Edward Manning, he took Holy Orders at Lucca in 1854.

On his return he became for a period Vice President of Saint Edmund's College, at that time the chief seminary for candidates for the priesthood in the south of England. Since childhood he had been filled with zeal for foreign missions, and he conceived the determination to found a great English missionary college to fit young priests for the work of evangelising non-Christians abroad. With this object he made a great fund-raising trip to America in 1863, from which he returned with £11,000.

St Joseph's Foreign Missionary College, Mill Hill Park, London, was opened in 1869. Vaughan also became proprietor of *The Tablet,* and used its columns vigorously for proclaiming his message. In 1872 he was consecrated Bishop of Salford; during his time in that office he established St Bede's College. In 1892 he succeeded Manning as Archbishop of Westminster, receiving the cardinal's hat in 1893. He was an ecclesiastic of remarkably fine presence and aristocratic leanings, intransigent in theological policy, and in personal character simply devout.

It was his most cherished ambition to see before he died an adequate Westminster Cathedral, and he laboured untiringly to secure subscriptions, with the result that its foundation stone was laid in 1895, and that when he died at the age of 71, the building was so far complete that a Requiem Mass was said there over his body before it was removed to its resting-place at Mill Hill Park. It was later moved to the cathedral.

In 1914, the Cardinal Vaughan Memorial School was founded in his memory in Holland Park, London.

The symbolic cross stands against a tree as Oxford University students rest by the roadside during their Easter pilgrimage to Walsingham in March 1964. Every hour, the party paused for prayer, taking a week to make the journey in time for Good Friday.

Mr. Tom Gillett, of Chorley, Lancs., (*above*) pictured in December 1968. Some 35 years earlier he had gained distinction as the founder of the *Chorley Catholic Bulletin*, a monthly publication selling 4,000 copies in 15 parishes. He not only edited it, but was its reporter and advertisement and circulation manager.

There was a rare treat for the children of the Holy Family primary school, Benfleet, Essex in June 1966, when they were able to watch husband and wife sculptors **Anne** and **Bernard David** (*right*) working on a one ton block of Portland stone at the school entrance.

Fr. Bernard Roe, rector of St. Etheldreda's, Ely Place, London – London's only pre-Reformation Catholic church – beside the Roman wall in the crypt of his church in January 1931. The bricks had been certified by the British museum to be of the third century.

Priests and nuns under the auspices of the Catholic Institute for International Relations taking part in a protest vigil outside the Brazilian embassy in London in May 1976. They were protesting about torture and imprisonment in Brazil, whose president was on a state visit.

Children from a convent school in south London have to walk to and from school wearing their gas masks in October 1939.

Going for a song: (*above left*) the great comic musical entertainer **Sir Harry Lauder** steals a kiss from the bride after the marriage in July 1930 of Miss Helen Cochrane to Mr. Harold Prior at St. John's RC church, Chorlton-cum-Hardy, Manchester.

Another society wedding was that of Mr. **Richard Everard Augustine Elwes**, (*above right*), son of the great tenor Mr. Gervase Elwes, and his wife Lady Winifride Elwes, to Miss Freya Sykes, daughter of the late Sir Mark Sykes MP. The wedding took place in Westminster Cathedral in November 1926, and the couple are pictured with the Bishop of Northampton, Monsignor Cary-Elwes, who was the uncle of the groom. Richard Elwes was the fifth son of Gervase Elwes, who achieved international fame as Gerontius in Cardinal Newman's and Elgar's *The Dream of Gerontius*. Richard became a leading High Court judge, and the couple's daughter, Polly Elwes, was a BBC announcer and interviewer on the *Tonight* programme in the 1950s.

In a jungle clearing in Manipur State, Burma, Fr. Nolan, an Army chaplain from Bradford, celebrates Mass on his jeep in November 1944.

A quiet corner of the Catholic Women's League Belgrave Service Women's Club near London's Victoria station gives women at war an opportunity to pray for peace in July 1942. The club was opened by Cardinal Hinsley.

Artists at work covering with glass mosaic the dome of the apse in the Chapel of Our Lady at Westminster Cathedral in March 1931. The artist on the right is identified as **Mr. Thomas Josey**.

Catholic men leaving the Friday Market, Walsingham, in procession during Walsingham Week in 1957.

CATHOLIC WRITER COMES HOME

The *Universe* photographer managed to slip aboard the great Cunard liner *S.S. Caronia* to capture this snapsot of the normally camera-shy writer A.J. Cronin with his wife and son, as they set sail from New York to England in June 1949. The writer and his family had been living in the USA, but had decided to return home permanently.

Archibald Joseph Cronin (19th July 1896 – 6th January 1981) was a Scottish novelist, dramatist, and non-fiction writer who was one of the most renowned storytellers of the 20th century. His best-known works are *The Citadel* and *The Keys of the Kingdom*, both of which were made into Oscar-nominated films. He also created the Dr. Finlay character, the hero of a series of stories that served as the basis for the long-running BBC television and radio series *Dr. Finlay's Casebook*.

Cronin was born at Rosebank Cottage in Cardross, Dunbartonshire, the only child of a Protestant mother, Jessie Cronin, and a Catholic father, Patrick Cronin, and would later write of young men from similarly mixed marriage backgrounds.

After their marriage, Cronin's parents moved to Helensburgh, where he attended Grant Street School. When he was seven years old, his father, a commercial traveller, died from tuberculosis. He and his mother moved back to her parents' home in Dumbarton, and she became the first female public health inspector in Scotland.

Cronin was not only a precocious student at Dumbarton Academy who won many prizes and writing competitions, but an excellent athlete and footballer. From an early age, he was an avid golfer, a sport he enjoyed throughout his life, and he loved salmon fishing as well.

The family later moved to Yorkhill, Glasgow, where he attended St. Aloysius' College. Due to his exceptional abilities, he was soon awarded a scholarship to study medicine at the University of Glasgow in 1914.

Cronin served as a Royal Navy surgeon during World War I before graduating from medical school. After the war, he trained at various hospitals before taking up his first practice in Tredegar, a mining town in South Wales.

In 1924, he was appointed Medical Inspector of Mines for Great Britain, and over the next few years, his survey of medical regulations in collieries and his reports on the correlation between coal dust inhalation and pulmonary disease were published.

Cronin drew on his experiences researching the occupational hazards of the mining industry for his later novels *The Citadel*, set in Wales, and *The Stars Look Down*, set in Northumberland. He subsequently moved to London and had a thriving practice on Harley Street.

Although noted for its deep social conscience, his work is filled with colourful characters and witty dialogue. In addition to stressing the need for tolerance, his works examine moral conflicts between the individual and society as his idealistic heroes pursue justice for the common man.

It was at university that he met his future wife, Agnes Mary 'May' Gibson, who was also a medical student. She and Cronin married on 31st August 1921. As a doctor, May worked in the dispensary while her husband was employed by the Tredegar General Hospital, and she also assisted him with his practice in London. When he became an author, she would proofread his manuscripts. Their first son, Vincent, was born in Tredegar in 1924. Their second son, Patrick, was born in London in 1926. Andrew, their youngest son, was born in London in 1937.

In the late 1930s Cronin moved to the United States with his family, living in Bel Air, California and Greenwich, Connecticut before eventually settling in New Canaan.

Ultimately, Cronin returned to Europe, residing in Storrington, West Sussex, Lucerne and Montreux, Switzerland for the last 25 years of his life and continuing to write into his 80s. He died on 6th January 1981 in Montreux, and is interred at La Tour-de-Peilz.

Members of the Armed Forces queueing outside Westminster Cathedral in March 1948 to file past the body of Cardinal Hinsley.

A general view of the garden party at St. Mary's College, Strawberry Hill, London, in September 1929, the last gathering of the 1929 Emancipation Congress.

Catholic Emancipation, or Catholic Relief, was a process in Great Britain and Ireland in the late 18th century and early 19th century which involved reducing and removing many of the restrictions on Catholics that had been introduced by the Act of Uniformity, the Test Acts and the Penal Laws. The Catholic Relief Act 1829 was passed by the Parliament of the United Kingdom on 24th March 1829, and received the Royal Assent on 13th April.

It was the culmination of the process of Catholic Emancipation in the United Kingdom, and in Ireland following a campaign on the issue by Irish lawyer and newly-elected Member of Parliament Daniel O'Connell.

World War Two hero **Group Captain Leonard Cheshire**, later Lord Cheshire, with his wife **Lady Ryder**, walk among the poppies near the Lochnagar Crater on the Somme in July 1989.

Sadly this picture is undated, but it shows **Archbishop McIntyre of Birmingham** blessing pilgrims as they passed through the market square, Lichfield, during the Midlands Catholic Pilgrimage to the town. John McIntyre was appointed Archbishop of Birmingham on 16th June 1921, and resigned on 17th November 1928, remaining Emeritus Archbishop until his death on 21st November 1935.

Clergy at Knott End, near Blackpool donned overalls and dressed as workmen during the Preesall Gala in August 1976. The Rev. R.F. Jackson, Vicar of Preesall *(centre)* drove a steam roller (borrowed from a friend), assisted by the Rev. H. C. Griffiths, United Reformed Church *(left)* and **Fr. Bernard Cochrane**, Catholic parish priest of St. Bernard's, Knott End. The venture was an extension of their normal monthly fraternal when they had an early service and breakfast together.

Lunchtime in the refectory of the newly completed £500,000 Prinknash Abbey, near Gloucester in April 1972. The new monastery, which became home to 37 Benedictine monks, replaced an old Tudor house, and boasted "central heating and shaver sockets in the cells" according to *The Universe*. The monastery was built by the monks themselves, with 2,500 tons of Cotswold stone.

The monks of Buckfast Abbey in solemn mood in December 1937, as they walked in procession from the abbey to the nearby burial ground, carrying the mortal remains of **Dom Edmond Broussard**, who had been the oldest member of the community.

Children escort Manchester Italian community's statue of Our Lady in the Whit Friday procession through the city in May 1948.

Archbishop McGrath of Cardiff, surrounded by members of his Chapter after his enthronement at St. David's Cathedral, Cardiff on Saturday 29th June 1940. Michael Joseph McGrath (1882 – 1961) was born in Kilkenny, and developed a strong interest in Celtic languages from an early age, gaining a B.A. in Irish from the National University of Ireland. He was later awarded an honorary D.Litt. He entered St. John's seminary, Waterford on 12th July 1908, and was ordained priest for the Diocese of Clifton.

He began his mission as a curate at Clifton cathedral, before moving to Fishponds, and then St. Nicholas in Bristol. After a period of ill health, he returned to work in the Menevia diocese, in Flint and later at Bangor.

He was transfered to Aberystwyth in 1928, where be became priest and Rector of the small Catholic college in the town, which greatly encouraged his passion for learning the Welsh language.

He was consecrated Bishop of Menevia on 24th September 1935, and became Archbishop of Cardiff in 1939, where he remained until his death on 28th February 1961.

Deep clouds filled the skies on Sunday 23rd July, 1950, as 14 crosses – each 13ft long and weighing 168lbs – were lined up before the entrance of St. Mary's Church, Glastonbury, opposite the ancient abbey ruins. It had rained torrentially all day Saturday and throughout Sunday morning, but as Bishop Rudderham of Clifton emerged from the church and stood to bless the crosses the sun burst through the clouds.

From that moment on the sun shone on the annual pigrimage that commemorated the martyrdom on Glastonbury Tor in November 1539, of Bl. Richard Whiting, last abbot of Glastonbury, and his companions.

More than 5,000 pilgrims were gathered in the rain for the ceremonies, which saw the crosses being blessed before being carried up the steep Tor, each cross accompanied by 40 men and a chaplain, with four men carrying the crosses in relays. Behind came the clergy and the bishop.

Near the summit the crosses were erected and the Stations were conducted by **Fr. Edgar Larway OFM**, the Guardian of Clevedon Friary.

A stirring sermon was delivered to the pilgrims by **Abbot Butler of Downside**, who said that, at the Reformaton, the breach with the Holy See had not been caused "by the will of our countrymen, but by the irresponsibility of their ruler.

"We can derive hope and encouragement today that our fellow countrymen are divided from us through a fault in which they had no share nor blame. They are our brethren by rights. Let us draw from this pilgrimage and from this historic place a new zeal and enthusiasm to show our country the real delights of the religion of Christ."

JFK REMEMBERED AT RUNNYMEDE

H.M. Queen Elizabeth II looks down on a suddenly shy little boy at Runnymede, Berkshire, on 14th May 1965. The young man is John Kennedy Junior, son of the late U.S. president, John F. Kennedy, who was assassinated on 22nd November 1963, just three days before John Junior's third birthday. The funeral procession actually took place on his birthday, 25th November 1963. While his father's flag-draped casket was being carried out from St. Matthew's Cathedral, Washington, young JFK Jr. stepped forward and, in an emotional and iconic image of the 1960s, gave his father a final salute.

The Kennedy family were at Runnymede in 1965 to see the Queen unveil a stone memorial *(pictured right)* to the late John F. Kennedy, on ground previously belonging to the Crown and now the property of the United States of America.

Standing halfway up the Cooper's Hill Slopes and overlooking Runnymede, the memorial is made of Portland stone to the design of G.A. Jellicoe, and is reached by treading a steep path of irregular granite steps, one for each year of Kennedy's life.

The inscription reads: "This acre of English ground was given to the United States of America by the people of Britain in memory of John F. Kennedy, born 19th May, 1917: President of the United States 1961-63: died by an assassin's hand 22nd November, 1963.

"Let every National know, whether it wishes us well or ill, that we shall pay any price, bear any burden, meet any hardship, support any friend or oppose any foe, in order to assure the survival and success of liberty": from the inaugural address of President Kennedy, January 1961."

Kennedy family members pictured above by *The Universe* photographer are *(from left)*: John Junior, Jacqueline Kennedy, daughter Caroline, and JFK's brothers the senators Robert and Edward Kennedy.

Remarkably, a photographer for *The Universe* followed allied and American troops up the beaches of Normandy with the invasion force of June 1944, recording many poignant images of Catholic troops. Here, **Fr. Jim McGovern**, a chaplain from Boston, gives Holy Communion during Mass which he celebrated at an altar on the sands.

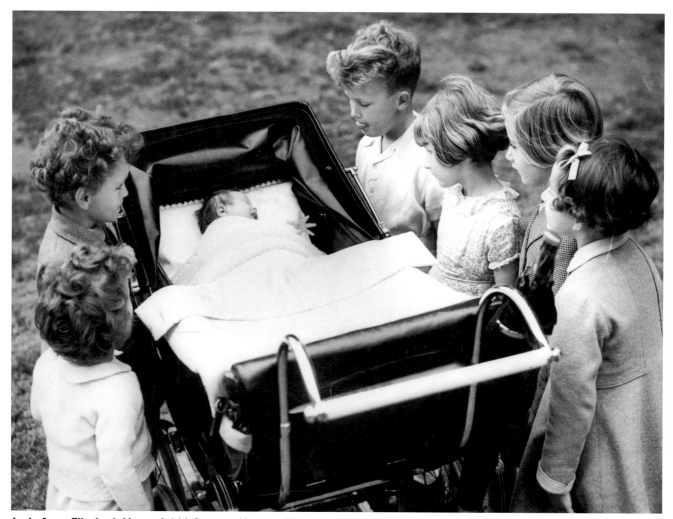

Lady Anne Elizabeth Howard, 14th Baroness Herries of Terregles, baby daughter of the Duke and Duchess of Norfolk, is the centre of attention during an outing in London's Hyde Park in July 1938. She was later to become Mrs. Anne Cowdrey, having married Baron Cowdrey of Tonbridge in 1985. Baron Cowdrey was of course the legendary English Test cricketer Colin Cowdrey, who married Anne after the death of his first wife.

Catholic Police Guild members at their annual Requiem for dead colleagues, held in Westminster Cathedral in November 1937.

His Eminence Cardinal Bourne inspects a car at the Armstrong-Siddeley works in Coventry in November 1927. The Cardinal used an Armstrong-Siddeley for long-distance travel, and *The Universe* reported that he: "showed great interest in the various stages of manufacturing the machine."

In some areas of the UK the absence of a nearby Catholic church meant that innovative ideas had to be utilised to make the Sacraments available, as this wonderful example of a 'motor chapel' pictured at Overton-on-Dee in North Wales in May 1957 illustrates.

A young hop worker greets **Bishop Amigo of Horsmonden** during his tour of the hop gardens of Kent in September 1931.

LAST MOMENTS OF BRAVE COMRADES

Father Leo Craig, right, and others attend to a wounded soldier after a land mine exploded. A photographer took this picture and left to retrieve more film. When he returned, all the people in the picture had been killed by the explosion from a second mine.

There were more than 30,000 US casualties of the Korean war, but one in particular is remembered by former students at the now-closed Aquinas College High School in Columbus.

Dominican **Father Leo Craig**, an Army captain and chaplain who was ordained in 1942, was given his first assignment at Aquinas College High School, where he taught for several years. But when the Korean War broke out, he volunteered as an Army chaplain and was sent to Fort Belvoir, Va., where he was assigned to the 1st Cavalry Division fighting in Korea.

In April 1951, the priest was near the city of Chunchon, South Korea. A truck in his outfit hit a land mine and Fr Craig left his own vehicle to tend to the wounded (*pictured above*).

While he was administering last rites to a

soldier, a second land mine exploded. A booby trap had been attached to that second land mine and all those around it were killed.

Gene Lauber, a 1946 graduate of Aquinas College High School, who had Fr Craig as a math teacher, also met up with the priest in Korea. Lauber, a draftee, was a staff sergeant in the same division as Fr Craig.

"I saw Father about three times. We talked about Aquinas. I served Mass for him on the front of a jeep. There were probably 15 to 20 guys that showed up for Mass out in the field. Fr Craig visited all the different outfits. You never knew when he was coming around. He was always on the move," said Lauber.

He described his former math teacher in Korea as "so extremely happy in what he was doing. He seemed extremely satisfied."

When Lauber got word of Fr Craig's

death, he wrote the school to give them the news.

Ray Tiburzio, who also graduated from the school in 1946 and had Fr Craig as a teacher for general math, describes the priest as "a very influential person in that part of my life."

"Father was a person who could bring out the best in you. He always found ways to keep us interested and always offered us encouragement to keep applying ourselves," he said.

"He was a gentle person, but he had a manner that could always demand your attention ... everyone in class thought the world of Father Craig. There were many priests and teachers we became more attached to, and he was one of them – his teaching methods, approach, enthusiasm, philosophy – he was one of the best, "said Tiburzio.

It was such a shame that this fantastically detailed study was in such a poor condition. It took several days to piece the flaking fragments together, and electronically restore the image to this level. In the early 1930s *The Universe* organised a series of pilgrimages to Rome and Lourdes for unemployed men from the UK and Ireland. Wearing a stole over a muffler and a much-worn trench coat, The Jesuit writer **Fr. C.C. Martindale** blesses the pilgrimage banners on the platform in Victoria station. The Irish contingent's banner is on the right. The driver and fireman of the pilgrimage train were among the spectators at the ceremony.

Cardinal Basil Hume and **Bishop Derek Worlock** in relaxed mood at the 1984 National Conference of Priests' conference.

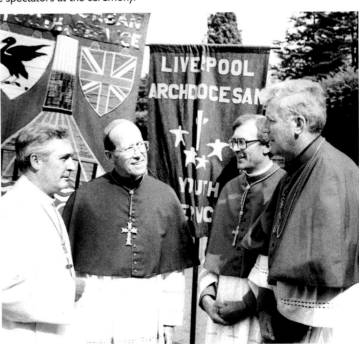

Archbishop Derek Worlock enjoys a conversation during the December 1984 Liverpool Archdiocesan Youth Service with *(left to right)* **Archbishop Thomas Winning** of Glasgow, **Bishop John Rawsthorne** (then Auxilliary Bishop in Liverpool, now Bishop of Hallam) and **Bishop** (later Cardinal) **Cormac Murphy O'Connor** of Arundel and Brighton.

All the boys in the two teams competing for the Merton (London) Primary Schools Cup at Merton Abbey in May 1967 gave their best as watching the game was Chelsea manager **Tommy Docherty.** The Gorbals-born player and manager had turned up with his wife to watch the match, as their son – also named Tommy – was playing for Sacred Heart, Raynes Park, which lost 2-1 to Holy Family, Marsden.

Father Philip Fletcher, Master of the Guild of Our Lady of Ransom, blesses one of the many street shrines erected in front of houses along the route of the Ransom procession in the Commercial Road parish in the East End of London in June 1926.

Archbishop John Carmel Heenan is welcomed at Euston station by his former secretary, **Bishop-Elect Worlock** of Portsmouth in September 1963 as the archbishop arrived in London to take over as Archbishop of Westminster.

Cardinal Bourne leads in nuns at the ceremony of enclosure at the Convent of the Poor Clares at Aston Hall, Hawarden, Flintshire, north Wales, in May 1932.

Bishop Holland of Salford *(left)* and **Fr. John Bergin**, parish priest of Mount Carmel, Salford, try to mediate on a cold January morning in 1969 as a group of travellers await their eviction from a temporary site on the outskirts of Manchester.

Lord and Lady Lovat leave Buckingham Palace after the commando leader was invested with the DSO and the MC in November 1942. Educated at Ampleforth, and a member of one of Scotland's most ancient and distinguished Catholic families, **Simon Christopher Joseph Fraser**, 15th Lord Lovat, was the 25th Chief of the Clan Fraser, and the 4th Baron Lovat in the Peerage of the United Kingdom. As a brigadier he led 1 Special Service Brigade onto Sword Beach on D-Day, wearing a white jumper with "Lovat" inscribed on the collar, and carrying an old Winchester rifle and a rolled umbrella. He also instructed his personal Piper Bill Millin to pipe them ashore, in direct defiance of military orders not to allow such actions in battle. The scene of him arriving to relieve Pegagus Bridge was immortalised in the movie *The Longest Day*.

One of Italy's most distinguished artists, **Commendatore C.T. Formilli**, was commissioned in February 1930 to decorate the whole of the interior of Brompton Oratory, in what *The Universe Catholic weekly* described as: "a 10 year task which will make the famous Oratory the most colourful church in England." The report concluded by mentioning that: "these pictures of Commendatore Formilli were obtained at great risk, having been taken on the scaffolding in the roof of Brompton Oratory."

A Lourdes Cure at Home

During the September of 1924 Mme. **Celestine Gardelle** (*pictured right*), a 53 year old French woman, developed pains in her head which quickly developed into a swelling that covered the whole of one cheek, virtually closing one eye. In the October and November of that year Dr. Haddon of Lezoux and Dr. Dionis of Clermont Ferrand both tried treatment without success. The swelling in fact increased rapidly. By the December Dr. Gillard a specialist also from Clermont Ferrand admitted the patient to his clinic. A portion of the growth was removed and examined, revealing that it was cancerous. Radiotherapy was tried in January 1925 by a Dr. Dechambre, but again with out success. By this stage frequent injections of morphia were needed so severe was the pain caused by the cancer. By February the swelling was so great that the eye was forced out of place and the swelling also moved to the left side of the nose as well.

It was then that Mme. Gardella's relatives made two novenas asking Our Lady of Lourdes to pray to God to cure her. On March 10th a third novena was begun. The injections continued in order to alleviate the pain. Water from the grotto at Lourdes was used as a dressing to the face, and Mme. Gardelle also drank some. The patient became delirious and the doctors informed her relatives that death was imminent. But on the 16th March Celestine slept naturally, on the 17th appeared better, by the 18th the pain disappeared, the swelling subsided and the eye returned to its natural position, the sight also being restored to normal. By April 1st Celestine Gardelle was back working on her farm. All four doctors who had seen and treated her declared her cured of the cancer. All the certificates were kept in the dossier at Lourdes, along with a technical description of the microscopic examination carried out on the cancer. Two of the certifying doctors were non-Catholics, one a Protestant and one Mohammedan.

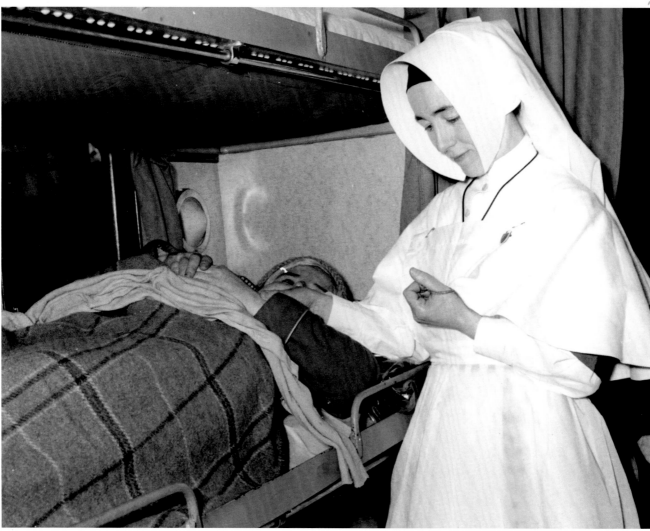

This photograph was taken by *The Universe*'s photographer in May 1964 aboard the ambulance coach of the National Lourde's Pilgrimage train, just prior to departure from Victoria Station. The nursing nun is taking the pulse of a sick pilgrim.

THE MIRACLE OF JOHN TRAYNOR

John Traynor was a native of Liverpool. His Irish mother died when he was quite young, but the faith which she instilled in her son remained with him the rest of his life. His injuries dated from World War I. As a result of wounds, Traynor's right arm was paralysed and the muscles atrophied. His legs were partially paralysed, and he was epileptic. Sometimes he had as many as three fits a day. By 1916, Traynor had undergone four operations in an attempt to connect the severed muscles of this right arm. All four operations ended in failure. By this time he had been discharged from the service. In April, 1920, his skull was operated on in an attempt to remove some of the shrapnel. This operation did not help his epilepsy, and it left a hole about an inch wide in his skull. The pulsating of his brain could be seen through this hole. A silver plate was inserted in order to shield the brain.

He lived on Grafton Street in Liverpool with his wife and children and was utterly helpless. He had to be lifted from his bed to his wheelchair in the morning and back into bed at night.

In July, 1923, Traynor heard that the Liverpool diocese was organising a pilgrimage to Lourdes. He had always had a great devotion to the Blessed Virgin and determined to join the pilgrimage. He took a gold sovereign which he had been saving for an emergency and used it as the first payment on a ticket. At first his wife was very much disturbed by the idea of her husband making such a difficult trip. His friends tried to talk him out of it and his doctor told him the trip would be suicide but Traynor had made up his mind, and there was no changing it. When his wife saw how much he wanted to make the trip, she decided to help him and in order to raise the money for the pilgrimage, the Traynors sold some of their furniture; Mrs. Traynor pawned some of her jewellry.

The trip was extremely trying, and Traynor was very sick. Three times, during the journey across France, the directors of the pilgrimage wished to take him off the train and put him in a hospital. Each time there was no hospital where they stopped, and so they had to keep him on board. He was more dead than alive when he reached Lourdes on July 22nd and was taken to the Asile. He had several hemorrhages during his six days there and a number of epileptic fits. So bad was his condition that one woman took it upon herself to write to his wife and tell her that there was no hope for him and that he would be buried in Lourdes.

Traynor managed to bathe in the water from the grotto nine times, and he attended all the ceremonies to which the sick are taken. It was only by sheer force of will that he was able to do this. Not only were his own infirmities a serious obstacle but the brancardiers and others in attendance were reluctant to take him out

for fear he would die on the way. Once he had an epileptic fit as he was going to the piscines. When he recovered, the brancardiers turned his chair to take him back to the Asile. He protested, but they insisted. They were forced to give in when he seized the wheel with his good hand and would not let the chair budge until it went in the direction of the baths.

On the afternoon of the 25th July when he was in the bath, his paralysed legs became suddenly agitated. He tried to get to his feet, but the brancardiers prevented him. They dressed him, put him back in his wheel chair, and hurried him to Rosary Square for the Blessing of the Sick, where he was blessed with the Blessed Sacrament.

Later that evening Jack awoke from his hospital bed and walked out of his room, to the amazement of those around him.

He proceeded to the Grotto and prayed the Rosary, not fully realising the significance of the events that were unfolding. By this time, word of his recovery was spreading among those in Lourdes and crowds were gathering wherever he went. Contemporary reports say Jack himself continued his pilgrimage as if nothing untoward had occurred.

Although the cure took place in 1923, the Medical Bureau waited till 1926 to issue its report. Traynor was examined again, and it was found that his cure was permanent. "His right arm which was like a skeleton has recovered all its muscles. The hole near his temple has completely disappeared. He had a certificate from Dr. McConnell of Liverpool attesting that he had not had an epileptic attack since 1923.

John pictured here in 1939 in Lourdes with his two sons Jack and Frank.

Aboard the Red Star liner Pennland at Southampton dock in June 1926, before their departure as delegates to the Eucharistic Congress in Chicago: *(from left)* **Rev. D. O'Mahoney** of St. Edmund's, Southampton, who saw the delegates off; **Mgr. D. O'Doherty**, Rector of the Irish College, Salamanca; **Rt. Rev. D. Munagouri**, Bishop of Tonkin, China; **Rt. Rev. Dr. Doubleday**, Bishop of Brentwood; **Rt. Rev. Dr. Heylam**, President of the Permanent Committee of the Eucharistic Congress; **Fidelis Von Shotzinger**, Abbot Primate of the Order of St. Benedict, and the **Very Rev. J.M. Arrese**, San Sabastian, Spain.

In the early morning light, **Princess Lowenstein-Wertheim** waits while the **Dr. Francis Mostyn**, Archbishop of Cardiff blesses her aircraft at the start of her ill-fated attempt to be the first woman to fly solo across the Atlantic. The flight, from Uphavon, Wilts, to Ottowa, Ontario, in the monoplane St. Raphael, took place on 31st August 1927, and the princess was accompanied by Capt. Leslie Hamilton and Col. F. F. Minchin. According to *The Universe*, on the morning of the flight the princess had: "left London by motor at 1am. At Devises she met the Archbishop, Fr. J. O'Reilly, Senior Chaplain to the Forces, and Fr. L. Valluet, and motored with them to the starting place, where Dr. Mostyn held a service under the wing and blessed the plane." The plane was last spotted "flying well" over Thurles, Co. Tipperary, but it never reached its destination, being assumed lost at sea. A plaque in her memory is on one of the walls at her family's church, St Raphael's Roman Catholic Church in Kingston, Surrey.

Two sixth formers, **Catherine Carline** and **Patsy Thomas**, of Adelphi House grammar school, Salford, laid a wreath at the Manchester cenotaph in January 1971 before leading a silent walk through the city in protest against the Abortion Act. The message on the wreath read: "In remembrance of the 85,000 babies aborted in 1970. RIP." More than 500 people, many of them teenagers, took part in the protest, which was organised by the National Youth Right to Life Campaign founded at Adelphi House. At the end of the walk, in Albert Square, the crowd sang carols.

Cardinal MacRory arriving at the new Cathedral of Christ the King at Mullingar to preside over its dedication in September 1936.

After heavy German bombing of London in April 1941, many churches in the city were left severely damaged. Among them was St. Dominic's, Homerton, where a bomber scored a direct hit on the church, and another fell bomb on the presbytery, where thankfully priests escaped with only minor injuries. In the morning after the attack, **Fr. Alphonse Arendzen** *(right)*, and his curate **Fr. Maurice Kelleher**, and a group of young parishioners sift through the debris.

Eoin O Mahony (1904 – 70) was one of modern Ireland's most colourful characters. Eoin was one the O Mahonys of Dun Locha, Douglas, County Cork, and was barrister, Knight of Malta, genealogist, raconteur and a world traveller. It was he who originated the annual O Mahony clan rally in 1955. He was once described as "a maker of epics, an interpreter of history, an incurable romantic, the avowed champion of lost causes, a sterling protagonist of the social values of rural Ireland with a mission of preservation of 'resistance to materialism'." He is pictured here as young man in the uniform of an officer of the Sovereign Order of the Knights of Malta.

In July 1931 Liverpool University conferred an honorary degree of Master of Arts *(Honoris Causa)* on **Wilhelmina Aspel** (Sister Imelda) in recognition of her having completed 25 years service as headmistress of Notre Dame Collegiate School, Everton valley, Liverpool, which at the time was the largest secondary school in Merseyside.

The congregation at Westminster Cathedral hold lighted candles during Mass on the Feast of the Purification in February 1936.

Cardinal William Godfrey

The man they called "Uncle Bill"

W illiam, Cardinal Godfrey (25th September 1889 – 22nd January 1963) was born in Liverpool. He leaned towards the priesthood from an early age, never taking another career into serious consideration. After studying at Ushaw College and the Venerable English College, he was ordained on the 28th October 1916 in Rome. He finished his studies in 1918, and did pastoral work in Liverpool until 1919. He taught Classics, Philosophy and Theology at Ushaw from 1918 to 1930, which was the same year he was raised to the rank of Domestic Prelate of His Holiness and rector of the English College. At the College, he was known affectionately to his students as "Uncle Bill".

In 1935, he was made a member of the Pontifical Commission to Malta, and he was in official attendance at the 1937 coronation of King George VI.

On the 21st November 1938 he was appointed Titular Bishop of Cius and the first Apostolic Delegate to Great Britain, Gibraltar and Malta.

Dr. Godfrey, who was the first papal representative to England since the Reformation, received his episcopal consecration the following December from Raffaele Cardinal Rossi, OCD, with Archbishop Luigi Traglia and Bishop Ralph Hayes serving as co-consecrators, in the chapel of the English College. He was chargé d'affaires of the Holy See to Poland in 1943, and was made Archbishop of Liverpool on 10th November 1953.

Pope Pius XII later, and not surprisingly, named Dr. Godfrey as Archbishop of Westminster on the 3rd December 1956. During his installation, Godfrey condemned Communism and professed his mission as returning England "back to the love of Christ". He also called for English Catholics to feed their pets less during Lent, and was vehemently opposed to birth control.

He was created Cardinal Priest of Ss. Nereo ed Achilleo by Pope John XXIII in the consistory of 15th December 1958. He only lived long enough to attend the first session of the Second Vatican Council in 1962. He died from a heart attack in London, at age 73, and is buried in Westminster Cathedral.

(Below) Attending the opening ceremony of St. John Vianney's Church, West Green Road, Tottenham, in April 1959.
(Top right) Leaving London for the consistory in Rome in December 1958.
(Bottom right) Dr. Godfrey in Liverpool in November 1958, saying goodbye to his ginger cat shortly after it was announced he was going to Westminster.

Daughters of the Cross of St. Wilfred's Convent, Chelsea, took part in the 'great daylight ARP test' which took place in London in June 1939. The *Universe* photographer caught this group receiving their final instructions from wardens.

Open air Mass at a makeshift altar for hop pickers in the fields of Kent, in September 1923. The Franciscan Fathers had established temporary mission centres in various parts of the hopfields, and were assisted by members of the Catholic Women's League.

Cardinal Hinsley in conversation with Queen Mary at a garden party in Hampton Court Palace, London in July 1938.

MASS RELICS FOUND IN LOFT

The Old Mass House at Egton, Yorks, where, in a little secret oratory, the **Ven. Fr. Nicholas Postgate** often celebrated Mass, had to be demolished in July 1928 on account of its extremely dilapidated condition.

The owner of the property, Mr. J. K. Foster, lord of the manor, though a non-Catholic, told *The Universe* that he regreted the disappearance of the historic building.

He gave instructions for a careful scrutiny to be made of anything which might have ecclesiastical associations and be deemed worthy of preservation, and invited *Universe* correspontent W.J. Ward to be present when the workmen began.

"Several interesting discoveries were made," said Ward.

"When the thatched roof was disturbed, a very much decayed bag, of linen and homespun, fell from it. Inside it were 23 silver coins in excellent condition, dating from Queen Elizabeth's reign to the reign of Charles II. The earliest is dated 1562, the latest 1649."

A careful examination of the thatch then revealed what was thought to be a collection-plate. It was of brown glazed earthenware, six and a half inches in diameter, with a pie-crust edge. For some reason or other the plate had been carefully preserved. At some time it had been broken into five pieces, and 13 holes were drilled in it, the pieces being then sewn together with shoemaker's waxed thread. The plate was covered with mud and thatch, which probably preserved the thread.

The most interesting find was the tabernacle. It was bricked and plastered up in a recess in the wall under the thatch.

Mr. Foster gave the plate, some of the coins, and the bag to the Catholic church at Egton Bridge, where they were preserved in an oak case made out of the flooring of the oratory.

The Old Mass House was built in the 16th century, and consisted of one living room and two bedrooms on the ground floor. Above these was the oratory, measuring 15 feet by 10 feet. Its greatest height is only five and a half feet.

The oratory was originally approached by a step ladder from the living room. There was a trap-door in the ceiling through which people assembled in the living room could see the priest celebrating Mass.

On the other side of the oratory was a secret trap-door through which the priest could escape in times of danger. A communicating door gave access to two other similar cottages, one of which stood on the site of the present Egton Church of England school.

When the oratory was discovered during the last century, the chalice, vestments, a rosary, and other things were found just as Fr. Postgate left them. Fr. Postgate was martyred at York on 7th August 1679. He was arrested at Littlebeck, near Whitby, whilst baptising a child at the house of Matthew Lyth, by Reeves, an exciseman. Reeves never received the £20 reward offered for information about priests, and he drowned himself in a small brook, which to this day is known as "Devil's Dump."

Fr. Postgate was born at Egton Bridge. He was educated at Douai, and came to England on 29th June 1630, about two years after his ordination. He was chaplain to Lady Dunbar at Saxton, and also served the Meynell and Saltmarshe families at Kilvington, near Thirsk.

He afterwards returned to Egton Bridge, and worked also at Ugthorpe, Pickering, and Whitby. He was 81 years of age when he was put to death.

BBC presenter **Patrick O'Donovan** *(left)* talks to Catholic writers and publishers **Frank Sheed** and **Maisie Ward**, who were to be the subject of his *The Way of Life* programme on Sunday, 27th January 1968. Making notes is the producer, **Fr. Agnellus Andrew**, who was a major figure in religious broadcasting at the time, having helped found the Catholic TV and Radio Centre at Hatch End, London.

On a scorching summer's day in August 1984, Ransomers lead their annual procession to the Church of the Annunciation, Walsingham.

Mohawk women lay flowers at the foot of a statue of **Kateri Tekakwitha** in Auriesville, N.Y., in 1956. The sainthood cause of the Native American maiden began in 1932. She was declared Blessed Kateri in 1980.

Business of the day starts at 9am for **Dr. Bernard Griffin**, as he dictates correspondence to one of his secretaries, Sr. M. Adrienne in 1943 shortly after being appointed Archbishop of Westminster. Born in Birmingham, on 21st February 1899, he was educated at Cotton College, Oscott, the Venerable English College and the Beda. He was ordained in 1924 and three years later became Secretary for 10 years to the Archbishop of Birmingham. He was Chancellor of the Diocese at 30 and a notable Administrator of its charitable homes. In 1938 he was made Auxiliary Bishop of Birmingham and during the war period succeeded Cardinal Hinsley as Archbishop of Westminster in 1943. Three years later, at the age of 47, he was created Cardinal. His links with social welfare helped him deal with the new post-war Labour Government as it carried out sweeping and widespread social reforms. He journeyed frequently abroad on Church affairs until stricken by illness which hampered his last years. He died on the 20 August 1956, at the age of 57.

A group at the opening and blessing by the Bishop of Nottingham of the new nursing home for the 'Blue Nuns' at Weedthorpe, Nottingham in September 1930. Included in the group are the Lord Mayor and Mayoress and the Sheriff of Nottingham.

Cardinal Bourne, photographed in June 1934 outside 120 Victoria Street, Westminster, after opening the new offices of the Westminster Catholic Federation. With him is Fr. Bernard Whelan, the clerical secretary of the Federation, which had been formed by the Cardinal: "with the object of enabling Catholics to take combined action in securing the due representation of Catholic interests in public bodies."

The Knights of St. Columba gather at Buckfast Abbey in August 1986 on their annual pilgrimage to celebrate the Immaculate Conception.

Monsignor Bruno Scott James was a remarkable, but somewhat eccentric, Walsingham priest. His friend, Right Reverend William Gordon Wheeler (formerly Bishop of Leeds), said that his memory of him: "enveloped in a black cloak, his head shorn, and with a Siamese cat perched on his shoulder, sitting on the steps of the Slipper Chapel and pouring out patristic pearls is a memorable one."

Fr. Bruno was born in Devonshire in 1906. He entered a monastery run by the Anglican Benedictines at Pershore (later at Nashdom), where he persued a deep interest in the early Church Fathers. According to Rev. Wheeler, Fr. Bruno was never quite comfortable in the Church of England, and during a visit to the Slipper Chapel in Walsingham, Fr. Bruno decided to take instruction from the Carthusians at Parkminster, and was eventually received into the Catholic Church at Sacred Heart, Hove.

He resided first at Downside Abbey, and then in the Certosa of Florence until the breakdown of his health compelled him to become a student again at Beda College, Rome, where he took instruction for the secular priesthood. After his ordination in 1935

he was appointed by the Bishop of Northampton, Dr. Youens, as first administrator of Walsingham, with a mandate to establish a shrine at Slipper Chapel.

During the period at Slipper Chapel (1935-1943), Fr. Bruno began an apostolate and inspired many seminarians to join him on pilgrimages around the country. He then moved back to Italy, where he was appointed by Pope Paul VI as canon of the Basilica of Santa Maria in Trastevere with the title of monsignor.

Failing health finally compelled Msgr. James to relinquish his duties as canon, and he returned to England. He died on March 16, 1984 at age 77, among friends in Brighton, and was buried at his beloved Downside Abbey.

During the Spanish civil war, Fr. Bruno travelled to the front line to say Mass, where the Marquis de Villada gave him his red beret to hang before the Shrine of Our Lady of Walsingham in the Slipper Chapel, in thanksgiving for his having served right through the war unscathed. Fr. Bruno is pictured hunouring the Marquis' request in March 1939.

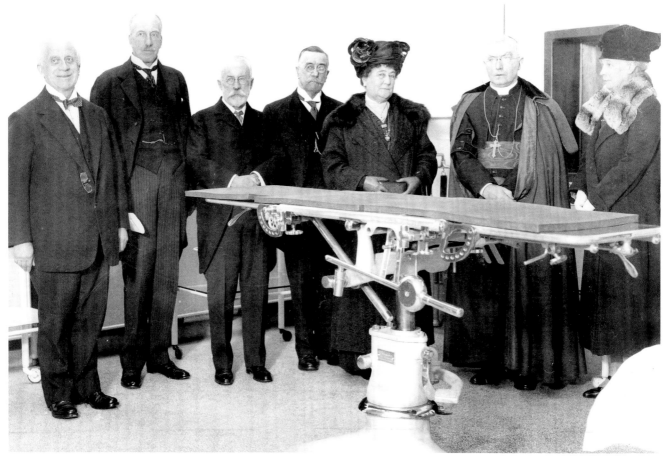

Cardinal Bourne of Westminster, pictured in an operating theatre with directors and surgeons of St. John's and St. Elizabeth's Hospital, London. The cardinal was opening a new wing at the hospital in November 1925.

Pope Pius XII inspects part of a consignment of 30,000lbs of canned meat, the gift of the Irish government for Italy's poor, in December 1950. In the period 1947-50, Ireland gave six million lbs of meat to Europe through NCWC War Relief Services. Pictured with the Holy Father are, from left, **Monsignor Ferdinando Baldelli**, President of the Pontifical Relief Commission, **Mgr. Andrew Landi**, chief of NCWC War Relief Services in Italy and **Mr. Patrick J. Walsh**, Irish Ambassador to the Holy See.

Like Rome, Ireland's ecclesiastical capital of Armagh is built on seven hills. This doesn't seem to have deterred **Cardinal Tomas O'Fiaich** from forsaking his car for a bicycle when he wanted to seek out grass roots opinions in April 1986. *The Universe* reported that locals referred to him as "the papal encyclical"!

The roof of the church of Notre Dame de France, Leicester Square, in the heart of London, being used as a playground in August 1927.

At the height of wartime, London Metropolitan and City police attend their annual Requiem Mass at Westminster Cathedral in October 1942 for deceased members, including those killed in air raids and other war activities. Over 600 policemen were present.

Frank Sheed was one of the most remarkable figures in 20th century English Catholicism, and was a central figure in the 'Catholic Intellectual Revival', an influential and loosely knit group of converts to the Faith, including authors such as G.K. Chesterton, Evelyn Waugh, Arnold Lunn, and Ronald Knox. An Australian of Irish descent, he graduated from Sydney University in Arts and Law, then moved in 1926, with his wife Maisie Ward, to London, where they founded the highly successful Catholic publishing company Sheed and Ward. A pioneer of the Catholic Evidence Guild, Frank could be found regularly taking to the CEG platform at Speakers' Corner in London's Hyde Park on a Sunday afternoon, answering questions on the Catholic faith and preaching to the crowds that gathered, as this rare photograph from the autumn of 1925 shows.

This remarkable photograph appeared in *The Universe* of the 24th April 1942. It was taken during Operation Archery, a British Combined Operations raid during World War Two against German positions on Vaagso (Vågsøy), Norway on the 27th December 1941.

The raid was conducted by British Commandos of No.3 Commando, two troops (platoons) of No.2 Commando, a medical detachment of No.4 Commando, a demolition party from 101 Troop (canoe) of No.6 Commando and a dozen Norwegians from Norwegian Independent Company 1. The action was supported by Royal Navy gunfire, led by the cruiser HMS Kenya, and Royal Air Force bombers and fighter-bombers.

The dawn landing was preceded by a naval bombardment and objectives went according to plan, except in the town of Vaagso itself. Opposition there was much stiffer than expected as unknown to the British, a gebirgsjäger (mountain) unit of experienced troops from the Eastern Front was there on leave. Their experience in sniping and street fighting caused Vaagso to develop into a bitter house-to-house battle.

At around 14:00 the Commandos started their withdrawal having destroyed four factories, the fish-oil stores, ammunition and fuel stores, the telephone exchange and various military installations. Much of the town was in flames. The Naval assault force of one cruiser and four destroyers had meanwhile sunk 10 vessels, some found in the act of being scuttled to prevent capture.

Central to the operation was the destruction of fish-oil production and stores which the Germans used in the manufacture of high-explosives. Another intention was to cause the Germans to maintain and increase forces in Norway which otherwise might be employed on the Eastern Front. No Royal Navy ships were lost, but the Navy suffered four men killed and four wounded.

The Commandos sustained 17 killed and 53 wounded, and the RAF had 8 planes downed. The Commandos accounted for at least 120 enemy killed and returned with 98 prisoners and a complete copy of the German Naval Code.

The raid was enough to persuade Adolf Hitler to divert 30,000 troops to Norway, upgrade coastal and inland defences, and send the battleship Tirpitz, the battlecruisers (or light battleships) Gneisenau and Scharnhorst, the pocket battleship Lützow, and the heavy cruisers Admiral Hipper and Prinz Eugen to Norway - a major diversion of effort and forces that could have had significant impact elsewhere. Hitler thought that the British might invade northern Norway to put pressure on Sweden and Finland.

The raid on Vaagso involved heavy street-to-street fighting, during which a 21 year old Catholic, Lieutenant Denis William Venebles Patrick O'Flaherty, was severely wounded. DWVP, as he was known, was an old boy of St. John's College, Southsea. Born in India, he was the only son of Lieut. and Mrs. O'Flaherty of St. Chad's Avenue, Portsmouth. He passed into the Royal Military Academy, Woolwich in 1938, and received his commission soon after the war began.

Our picture shows the young Royal Artillary Commando officer being rushed to an advanced dressing station to have his wounds tended to. Lieut. O'Flaherty was later awared the D.S.O. for his bravery during the raid. The leader of the raids, Brig. Haydon, also a Catholic, received a bar to his D.S.O.

Wembley's huge stadium was bathed in summer sunshine as 90,000 Catholics packed the stands and terraces on Sunday 1st October 1950 for Mass to mark the conclusion of the Hierarchy Centenary Congress. The scene came at the close of a week of events commemorating the day in 1850 when Pope Pius IX restored to territorial sees in England and Wales the bishops whose long line, stretching from the days of Gregory and Augustine, had been severed at the Reformation. In his message to Wembley Stadium the Holy Father said that: "The zeal of the hierarchy and of a loyal, industrious clergy and laity has indeed crowned the fond hopes of Pius IX with the joy of fulfilment."

More than 1,000 people took part in a Good Friday Interdenominatonal open air 'Act of Witness' service held on St. George's Plateau, Liverpool, some time in the early 1970s, narrated by film and television star, Liverpool-born John Gregson.

Pictured (left to right) are the Bishop of Liverpool, Rt. Rev. Stuart Blanch; The Archbishop of Liverpool, Most Rev. G.A. Beck; Mr John Gregson; and the Rev. R. Kissack, Chairman of the Liverpool Methodist District. Unfortunately the picture is undated, so we are hoping readers can give us some idea of when exactly it was taken.

John Gregson (15th March 1919 – 8th January 1975) was born as Harold Thomas Gregson in Wavertree, Liverpool, of Scottish descent, where he was educated at St Francis Xavier School. He met his wife, the actress Thea Gregory, when they were appearing together in rep. at Perth in 1946 and they were married in London in 1947. They had three daughters and three sons.

John appeared in 40 films between 1948 and 1971 and on television from 1960 until his death. He died suddenly from a heart attack in Porlock Weir, Somerset, aged 55.

Bernard Marmaduke Fitzalan-Howard, 16th Duke of Norfolk, pictured in July 1936 after the 28-year-old premier Duke of England announced he was to marry the Hon. Lavinia Strutt, 20-year-old daughter of Lord Belper. The Duke had to divide his time between organising his wedding and planning the coronation of King George VI.

British Prime Minister **Mr. Neville Chamberlain** and his wife Anne de Vere Cole, pictured for The Universe in January 1939, on their visit to the Vatican for a private audience with Pope Pius XI. His Holiness had suffered a serious heart attack just hours before the audience, but refused to cancel and greeted his guests personally. He died three weeks later.

The Rt. Rev. Hugh Lindsay, Bishop of Hexham and Newcastle, making a point as he performed the opening ceremony at a workshop at Minsteracres Retreat Centre, Nr. Consett, Northumberland, in July 1980. To the left is the Rector of Minsteracres, Fr. Luke Magee.

A group of nuns at an undisclosed location in London in October 1942 are given a demonstration of resuscitation techniques at a building damaged by an air raid. The nuns were in training to help offer medical assistance to victims of daily bombing raids by the Luftwaffe.

A rainy evening at Speakers' Corner in London's Hyde Park, and a Catholic Evidence Guild speaker is silhouetted against a background of trees and a lowering sky in June 1969. Founded in 1918, the Westminster branch of the Guild is still thriving today.

Bishop Philbin of Down and Connor *(wearing hat)* is interviewed by newsmen behind a barbed wire barricade manned by British troops as the bishop toured the Catholic Falls Road area of Belfast in August 1969.

Washington DC. Irish Ambassador Thomas J. Kiernan calls at the White House on March 15 1963,
for the envoy's annual St. Patrick's Day delivery of good wishes - and potted shamrocks.
He called two days early because the president was leaving later that afternoon for Palm Beach, Florida.

AN IRISH REBEL TALE

James P. Gannon, author of *Irish Rebels, Confederate Tigers*, pictured in 1999 at the grave of Colonel William Monaghan, who was killed in a battle at Shepherdstown, W.Va., on Aug. 25, 1864.

Gannon's book is the first study ever undertaken of the 6th Louisiana Volunteer Infantry, one of the fighting Louisiana Tiger regiments!

This predominantly Irish unit was raised in New Orleans shortly after secession and saw action in virtually every major battle in the Eastern Theater.

The Louisianans opened their service with Stonewall Jackson in the Shenandoah Valley Campaign of 1862, where they experienced bitter fighting at Port Republic and suffered heavy losses. After fighting in the Seven Days' Battles at Gaines Mill and Malvern Rill, they tramped north to defend the unfinished railroad cut at Second Manassas, crossed into Maryland, and died by the score in the corner of the bloody Cornfield at Sharpsburg.

After more Louisianans fell in the Fredericksburg and Chancellorsville Campaigns, the Irishmen marched north to Gettysburg, where they assaulted East Cemetery Hill on July 2, 1863.

Under strength and exhausted, they persevered through the disaster at Rappahannock Station, and the freezing cold winter weather of the Mine Run Campaign.

The spring of 1864 opened with the battles of the Wilderness and Spotsylvania, where in the latter combat the Louisianans fought in the swirling hell of the "Mule Shoe".

Called back into the Valley with Jubal Early, the 6th Louisiana marched to the very gates of Washington before suffering a string of devastating defeats at Third Winchester, Fisher's Hill, and Cedar Creek. By the time the proud Regiment reached the trenches of Petersburg, its original complement of almost 1,000 soldiers had been whittled down to less than 75 men.

Few were left when General Robert E. Lee surrendered his army at Appomattox Court House in April 1865.

CARDINAL JAMES A. HICKEY

Cardinal James A. Hickey made Catholic education and service to the poor two of his top priorities during his years in the nation's capital. "He always showed the face of the church to the poor," Cardinal Theodore E. McCarrick of Washington told *The Washington Post*, in an obituary tribute in October 2004.

"For me, that ... really summarized the whole kind of man and whole kind of vision Jim Hickey had."

In a telegram to Cardinal McCarrick responding to the news of Cardinal Hickey's deah after a long illness, Pope John Paul II recalled Cardinal Hickey's "unfailing commitment to the spread of the Gospel, the teaching of the faith and the formation of future priests."

A statement by President George W. Bush called the late prelate "an inspirational leader who brought comfort to the sick and hope to those in need. He was a caring and compassionate man who for 20 years led the archdiocese with great dignity and conviction", Bush said.

In other messages of condolence, New York Cardinal Edward M. Egan called Cardinal Hickey "a devoted pastor of souls whose learning and wisdom did immense good throughout his years as priest and bishop."

Outwardly Cardinal Hickey was a quiet, soft-spoken man of faith, but behind the scenes he was a tireless worker and skilled administrator who built networks of church and community partnerships to serve the poor and to provide better educational opportunities for children.

When he was named Washington's new archbishop in 1980, succeeding Cardinal William Baum, challenges that then-Archbishop Hickey would face – and develop outreach for – in the years ahead included rising homelessness, a growing elderly population and a need for new parishes and schools as the area's increasingly diverse population grew steadily in outer regions of the metropolitan area.

Washington also was seeing a tide of Spanish-speaking immigrants coming into the area as they fled war and poverty in Central America.

The archdiocese's tie with that region became even stronger when in December of that year, laywoman Jean Donovan and Ursuline Sister Dorothy Kazel – whom then-Bishop Hickey of Cleveland had commissioned to serve as missionaries in El Salvador – were murdered along with two other American churchwomen in that war-torn land. In his small chapel, he always kept photos of his murdered friends, as a reminder of how they gave their lives to serve the poor.

A man who grew up in the small town of Midland, Mich., became a force for change in the nation's capital, a man who befriended presidents and diplomats but who felt most at home bringing the sacraments to people at parish Masses and visiting Catholic schoolchildren in their classrooms.

Washington's archbishop, who was made a cardinal in 1988, oversaw the establishment of 16 new parishes or missions; food and shelter programs for the homeless; homes for the frail elderly and residences for active seniors; and numerous educational, medical and legal services for immigrants and the working poor.

"I was always convinced that to be a good priest you had to be concerned for the poor and forgotten. People in those conditions need respect, they need love," the cardinal once said.

As a boy, he had seen how his father, a Depression-era dentist, provided free care for the poor. As archbishop of Washington, Cardinal Hickey convened a group of doctors in his living room to start the Archdiocesan Health Care Network.

By his retirement in 2000, that network of volunteer doctors, nurses and dentists, with participating local hospitals, provided $2 million in free health care to more than 3,000 clients annually.

To deal with major financial challenges confronting Catholic schools he raised $25 million, mostly for scholarship assistance, through a capital campaign in the 1980s.

He started a Faith in the City programme which had revitalisation of the city's Catholic schools as its central focus, and he oversaw the establishment of several new schools and the expansion of existing ones

across the archdiocese.

"We didn't leave the city," the cardinal said. "We consider the city and its children very precious. ... To me, Catholic education is the most valuable gift we can share."

In the mid-1980s, under his leadership, the Archdiocese of Washington established one of the first and most comprehensive child protection programs in the country, to address the problem of child abuse.

Another hallmark of Cardinal Hickey's tenure was his promotion of vocations. He once described his own vocation as "the story of a happy, happy priest who simply wants to tell the whole world that the priesthood of our church is a truly important way to serve God, and a way of life on which our Catholic people – and indeed our world – depend so much."

A Michigan native, James Aloysius Hickey was born on Oct. 11, 1920, in Midland. He was ordained a priest of the Diocese of Saginaw, Mich., on June 15, 1946, and served there as a pastor, vocations director and seminary rector.

He became an auxiliary bishop of Saginaw in 1967. From 1969 to 1974 he was rector of the North American College, the U.S. seminary in Rome. In 1974 he was named bishop of Cleveland.

Cardinal Hickey held doctorates in canon law from the Lateran University in Rome and in theology from the Angelicum, also in Rome. He received honorary degrees from nine U.S. colleges and universities.

For the Holy See, Cardinal Hickey served on the Pontifical Council for the Family and on four congregations: for sainthood causes, clergy, Catholic education and institutes of consecrated life and societies of apostolic life.

He was a member of numerous committees of the U.S. bishops' conference and chaired five of them: priestly formation in 1968-69; pastoral research and practices, 1974-77; doctrine, 1979-81; human values, 1984-87; and North American College, 1989-91 and 1994-97.

He died at the Jeanne Jugan Home of the Little Sisters of the Poor in Washington, D.C., at age 84. Following a funeral Mass at the National Shrine of the Immaculate Conception, he was buried in St. Francis Chapel at St. Matthew's Cathedral.

When asked by *The Washington Post* in 1989 what he would like people to say about him after his death, the Cardinal replied, "First, I'd like them to say that he was always loyal to his Church. Second, that he was a friend to Catholic education. And third, if they don't want to say the first two, at least I hope they would chisel on the stone, 'He served the poor.'"

CHANGING TIMES, CHANGING HABITS

(Left) Sisters Hospitaller of the Sacred Heart of Jesus, a Spanish order based in Brompton, south west London, changed their old habit, on the right, for the version on the left in the late 1970s. Pictured (from left) are **Sr. Rose, Sr. Cecilia** and **Sr. Nieves**. The habit in the centre is the nursing habit of the order. (Above) Similar changes took place to the habit of the Sisters of Charity.

Members of the Society of St. Vincent de Paul at the 150 year anniversary celebrations of the organisation in Dublin's Society Hall, in October 1983.

On a foggy morning in February 1969 a squad of Young Crusaders formed by students at the Capuchin Franciscan juniorate, Childer Thornton, Wirral, prepare to distribute *The Universe* to local parishes. The Young Crusaders was a collaboration between *The Universe* and seminarians to give them direct experience of parish life, and at the same time to promote the apostolate of the Catholic press.

George Patrick Dwyer (25th September 1908 – 17th September 1987), pictured in May 1964 on a pastoral visit as Bishop of Leeds to Bentham, Yorks. The bishop is pictured with Fr. Michael Killeen, parish priest of St. Boniface's, Bentham, and parishioner Mrs. Huban with her two year old son Michael and, in the bishop's arms, her eight months' old son Mark.

George Dwyer was educated at St Bede's College, Manchester, then at the Venerable English College, Rome. Following postgraduate studies, he returned to St Bede's as a member of the teaching staff before joining the Catholic Missionary Society as vice-superior in 1947.

He also edited the *Catholic Gazette* for four years until his appointment as Superior of the Catholic Missionary Society in 1951.

He was ordained bishop on 24th September 24, 1957, following his appointment as Bishop of Leeds, and went on to become Archbishop of Birmingham in October 1965.

After the death of John Carmel Heenan in 1975, Dwyer was seen by some as a natural successor as Archbishop of Westminster. However, he felt that at 67 his age was too great for him to be considered. He was, however, elected president of the Bishops' Conference during the first three years of Basil Hume's archbishopship, the only bishop ever to hold that position who was not also Archbishop of Westminster.

Throughout the Spanish Civil War, *The Universe* followed the rest of the Catholic Church in supporting the nationalist forces of General Franco. After calling for financial help from its readers, *The Universe* was able to send large amounts of aid to Spain, including food, clothing and several field ambulances. In October 1936 three "Universe" lorries containing medical supplies for "the anti-reds" as the national troops were called, arrived at the Burgos Red Cross headquarters. There to meet them were Catholic contacts in Spain, including nuns working as medics, and Count Vallellano *(far right)*, Spanish Red Cross chief.

Cardinal Bourne pictured during a visit to discuss working conditions with mill workers in Preston in March 1931.

Leaders and members of St. Augustine's Brownie and Guide Pack pictured at the laying of the foundation stone for St. Joseph's Catholic Church, Weymouth, Dorset in 1932.

Evacuated children from a north London convent school in September 1939 are pictured at prayers with their teacher, following morning roll-call at their new school "somewhere in the Midlands".

The Marquess MacSwiney, President of the Irish Knights of Malta, inspecting the knights' newly-formed ambulance unit in the grounds of the Bishop's Palace at Killarney in October 1939.

Sister Rosanna *(left)* and **Sister Laurentia** arrive with a selection of books, films and other teaching aids for a new bookshop that their order had opened in Birmingham in November 1964.

Described by *The Universe* as "the first picture of nuns in this country wearing gas masks", these unlucky sisters were snapped whilst taking part in an ARP course for women at Stoke Newington ARP training school in July 1938.

The monks of Fort Augustus Abbey, on the shores of Loch Ness, ignore legends of monsters to go fishing on 23 February 1935.

In 1934 **Cardinal MacRory**, the Irish Primate, paid a visit to the shrine of Our Lady of Montallegro, Rappalo, before he embarked at Marseilles as Papal Legate to the Eucharistic Congress being held in Melbourne. His Eminence is pictured using the new cable car to visit to the mountain shrine.

Mr John F Kavanagh, head of the sculpture department of the Leeds School of Art, was awarded a £750 contract in February 1941 for the memorial in Galway to Fr Tom Burke, famous Irish Dominican, whom Pope Pius IX described as "the prince of preachers." Mr Kavanagh, aged 39, comes from Cork. His bronze of Cardinal Hinsley was exhibited at the Royal Academy a few years ago. The memorial will be erected in the new public park, close to Fr. Burke's Galway home.

The body of **His Eminence John, Cardinal D'Alton**, lies in state in St Patrick's Cathedral, Armagh, in 1963. An all-night vigil was kept by the men of Armagh. Cardinal D'Alton succeeded Cardinal MacRory as Archbishop of Armagh and Primate of All Ireland in 1946.

Bishop Barrett follows the relics of Blessed Cuthbert Mayne in a pilgrimage in the martyr's honour at Launceston, Cornwall, on Sunday 17 June 1932. **Bishop John Patrick Barrett** was born in Liverpool in 1878 and became Auxiliary Bishop of Birmingham in 1926. He was appointed Bishop of Plymouth diocese on the 7th June 1929, and he died on the 2nd November 1946. St Cuthbert Mayne was a convert to the Catholic faith who was martyred in horrific fashion in 1577. He was canonised by Pope Paul VI in 1970. Visitors to St. Cuthbert Mayne RC church, St. Stephen's Hill, Launceston, can see his shrine, which includes a relic of the saint's skull and the "Inspeximus" issued by the Crown to Sir George Carey in 1581, giving details of the charge against Cuthbert Mayne. The latter provides evidence that the saint suffered martyrdom solely because of his religion.

A solemn moment of reflection and prayer at the gravesides of **Cardinal John Henry Newman** and Ambrose St. John during an annual pilgrimage to the site at the cemetery at Rednal Hill near Birmingham in 1925. It was Newman's profound wish that he be buried with his lifelong friend Ambrose St. John, who converted to Catholicism at the same time as Newman. On the 22nd January 1991 Pope John Paul II confirmed the judgment of the Congregation for the Causes of Saints that John Henry Newman had practiced the theological and moral virtues "to a heroic degree", a pronouncement that has opened the cause for his sainthood.

Bishop William Gordon Wheeler is enthroned at Leeds Cathedral on 27th June 1966.

Catholics gather and kneel to recite a Rosary for peace in London's Hyde Park on 10 September, 1960.

Cardinal Godfrey of Westminster poses with La Sagesse nuns at Golders Green, on the occasion of their golden jubilee in October 1959.

In July 1963 *The Universe* was invited on location in France to report on the filming of a new Fred Zinnerman film *Behold a Pale Horse*, starring **Gregory peck** and **Omar Sharif**. Peck played a former resistance leader, exiled to the Pyrenees, and Sharif a priest making a pilgrimage to Lourdes. The *Universe* photographer snapped this unique picture of Zinnerman rehearsing a sequence with the two stars, with the Lourdes churches in the background.

Nearly 2,000 Catholics of the West Country went on pilgrimage in June 1931 to Glastonbury, in memory of the last Abbot of Glastonbury, Abbot Whiting, and two of his monks, who were hanged on Glastonbury Tor. At the foot of the cross set up near the spot where they met their death, the pilgrims were addressed by **Dom Benedict Steuart, OSB**, Prior of Prinknash.

Members of the Garda Siochona, who were in Rome for the 60th anniversary of the Irish police, meet with **Pope John Paul II** in April 1982.

Singer **Frankie Vaughan** (*rear centre*) pays a visit to Catholic youngsters in Easterhouse, Glasgow in August 1987, to see for himself how the multi-faith centre he had helped establish 20 years previously was faring. Frankie Vaughan changed the face of Easterhouse in the late 1960s. Concerned by the gang warfare he saw among the young people, he co-ordinated a successful weapons amnesty. He gave money to set up the Easterhouse Project for local youngsters, donating the proceeds from his concert takings at Glasgow Pavillion. During his visit he met **Fr. Paul Stewart** from the neighbouring parish of St. Benedict, who was one of the project's trustees.

Pupils hard at work in a classroom at Worth Abbey School, Crawley, Sussex, in June 1967.

In September 1933 *The Universe* organised a pilgrimage to Rome for unemployed men from Great Britain and Ireland. On their arrival at St. Peter's *(above right)* they were granted an audience with the Pope. Large cheers greeted their return at Victoria station, London, *(below)* many of them holding the special commemorative medals given to them by *The Universe*. The men also carried large, lovingly hand-painted banners on the trip, one of which has survived *(above)* and, though somewhat battered after 75 years, it hangs proudly today in the office of *Universe* CEO Joseph Kelly.

Monks from Nunraw vote at Garvald village, East Lothian, in May 1983.

Members of the Catholic Missionary Society pose with their motor chapel, at Grantham, Lincolnshire in September 1939.
Left to right: Fr. Walls, Fr. Beck, Canon Arendzen, Fr. Dudley, Fr. L. Arendzen and Fr. Foley.

More than 3,000 people attended the Independence Day party given by the American Ambassador, Mr. Lewis Douglas, at his embassy residence in Princes Gate, London in July 1947. the *Universe* photographer was on hand to capture this study of **Cardinal Griffin** of Westminster chatting with Dolores Grey, star of the show *Annie get Your Gun*, and Sharman Douglas.

Preparing themselves for the ordeal of invasion, men of the Allied Forces discuss their spiritual problems with **Fr. Clement Tigar SJ**, during a weekend retreat at Campion House, Osterley, Middlesex, in April 1944. Thirty years later, on 4th October 1974, *The Universe* reported that Fr. Tigar was "celebrating the golden jubilee of his ordination quietly by offering Mass at St. Mary's, Ryde, Isle of Wight". Fr. Tigar was appointed to succeed Campion House's founder, Fr, Edmund Lester, in 1935. In his 31 years at Osterley he saw 637 of his former pupils ordained, 16 per cent of all priests in England and Wales at the time. During the war he held regular retreats for the troops at Campion House. Some of his retreatants even returned from the war to study for the priesthood. He is pictured above with troops on retreat just before the D-Day invasion of France. Fr. Tigar was also widely known for his devotion to the Forty Martyrs and was for many years the leading advocate of their canonisation cause, and wrote an influential book on the subject.

"I love visiting prisons," **Cardinal Hume** said following a two and a half hour visit to Pentonville in September 1977. The cardinal is pictured being introduced to staff by the Governor, Mr. Roland Adams.

Bishop Holland of Salford dedicating a new coronary care ambulance after it had been presented to Hope Hospital, Salford in October 1972.

Pilgrims kneel and kiss the grave of **Blessed** (later saint) **John Kemble**, at Welsh Newtown in August 1961. John Kemble was born at Rhydicar Farm, St. Weonard's, Herefordshire, in 1599, into a prominent local Catholic family which boasted four other priests. He was ordained a priest at Douai College, France, on 23rd February 1625, and returned to England on 4th June 1625 as a missioner in Monmouthshire and Herefordshire. Little is known of his work caring for the sustenance of his flock for the next 53 years. The conditions for Catholics had eased from the ferocious persecution of the Elizabethan period, but the priest performed his ministry discreetly. What we can deduce from his later treatment was the esteem and affection he was held in locally. He was falsely implicated in the Titus Oates plot of 1678. The then 80 year old priest was sentenced to be hung, drawn and quartered at Hereford, but it was agreed, because of his frailty, to allow him to die before disembowelling and quartering of his body took place. The execution took place at Widemarsh Common, Hereford, on 22nd August, 1679, but the executioner so botched his task that the ageing Fr. Kemble hung on the gallows for more than half an hour before being declared dead. One of his hands is preserved at St. Francis Xavier, Hereford, and his body lies in the (C of E) churchyard of St. Mary's, Welsh Newtown, near Hereford, to which Catholics still make an annual pilgrimage.

The entire episcopate of England and Wales pictured at their Low Week meeting at St. Edmund's College, Ware, in May 1941. Front row (*l-r*): Bishop Shine (Middlesbrough), Archishop Amigo (Southwark), Archbishop Downey (Liverpool), Cardinal Hinsley, Archbishop Williams (Birmingham), Archbishop McGrath (Cardiff), and Bishop Doubleday (Brentwood). Second row (*l-r*): Bishop Hannon (who had been consecrated the day before as Bishop of Menevia), Bishop Flynn (Lancaster), Bishop McNulty (Nottingham), Bishop Moriarty (Shrewsbury), Bishop Lee (Clifton), Bishop Barrett (Plymouth), Bishop Dey (Ordinary of H.M. Forces), Bishop Poskitt (Leeds), Bishop King (Vicar Capitular, Portsmouth), Bishop Parker (Northampton), Bishop McCormack (Hexham and Newcastle) and Bishop Marshall (Salford).

Cardinal Hinsley stands before the Walsingham beacon, as he gives his blessing to young pilgrims in Common Place in July 1938.

Mr. and Mrs. G.K. Chesterton, pictured arriving for Sunday Mass at Westminster Cathedral, in June 1931, on the day that the Westminster Catholic Federation celebrated its silver jubilee.

The Bishop of Dromore blesses the new grotto for St. Mary's Church, Leitrim in June 1929.

Cardinal McRory, Primate of All Ireland, second from left, with **Bishop Mageean** of Down and Connor, making the ascent of Slieve Patrick, Saul, Co. Down in June 1938, to bless a giant statue of St. Patrick.

The bombing of Our Lady of Victories, Kensington, London, didn't stop **Fusilier Tom Dowling** and **Miss Martha Coogan** from being married there on 14th September 1940. **Fr. Pinn**, who performed the ceremony, is pictured guiding the couple from the ruined church.

A magnificent new church was begun in June 1928 at Douai Abbey, Woolhampton, Berkshire, for which the Bishop of Portsmouth, **William T. Cotter**, laid the foundation stone.

Workers for the Catholic Women's League pictured in November 1943, just after arriving in North Africa and the Middle East for social work. Front row (l-r) Miss Goodman; Miss Mawson and Mrs. Borton; second row (l-r) Miss Seagrave-Daly, Miss Whyte and Miss Feeny.

Sisters Gabriel and Patricia of the Sisters of Charity, Cardiff, give a push to two boys from the city's Mostyn School in January 1973. Pupils made four of the carts for the sisters to give to needy families in their care.

Monsignor Filmer, Master of the Guild of Our Lady of Ransom, leads a procession through the streets of London in May 1943.

Peter F. Anson, co-founder of the Apostleship of the Sea, takes a break at Macduff Harbour on the Moray Firth, in September 1958.

Cardinal Basil Hume stands at the centre of the great circular Assembly Hall of Church House, London where he gave an historic address on Christian unity to the Synod of the Church of England in February 1978, the first time that an Archbishop of Westminster had addressed the Synod.

CARDINAL BOURNE
CARDINAL 11TH SEPT 1903 – 1ST JANUARY 1935

Born in Clapham to an English Civil Servant father and an Irish mother, **Francis Bourne** entered St. Cuthbert's College in Ushaw in 1867 and then St. Edmund's College in Ware in 1877. He joined the Order of Friars Preachers (Dominicans) in Woodchester but left in 1880 to attend St. Thomas' Seminary in Hammersmith, from where he went to study in France, at Saint-Sulpice Seminary in Paris and the University of Leuven in Belgium.

He was ordained to the priesthood on 11th June 1884, and then did pastoral work in Blackheath, Mortlake, and West Grinstead until 1889.

Bourne was rector of the House of Studies at Henfield Place from 1889 to 1891, at which time he began teaching at St. John's Seminary in Wonersh.

He became rector on 14th March 1896. He was raised to the rank of Domestic Prelate of His Holiness by Pope Leo XIII in 1895.

On 27th March 1896 Bourne was appointed Coadjutor Bishop of Southwark and Titular Bishop of Epiphania in Cilicia. He received his episcopal consecration the following May from Herbert Cardinal Vaughan, in St. George's Cathedral.

Bourne later became Bishop of Southwark on 9th April 1897, and was named Archbishop of Westminster on 11th September 1903.

In defiance of the then governmental law banning Eucharistic processions, Cardinal Bourne gave the benediction from the loggia of Westminster Cathedral in 1908. He also responded to Ramsay MacDonald's call for an English Catholic prelate's interpretation of Pius XI's encyclical *Quadragesimo Anno*, which forbade Catholics from being Socialists, by stating: "There is nothing in the encyclical which should deter Catholics from becoming members of the ritish Labour Party."

However, the Cardinal continued to warn Catholics to be cautious of the "erroneous principles which sometimes affect parties."

Bourne was not overly supportive of interfaith dialogue, and desired to see the United Kingdom adopt the Catholic faith as its official religion.

He died after a year's illness in his archiepiscopal residence in London, at age 73. He was buried at his alma mater of St. Edmund's College, in the chapel he established in memory of the College's members who died during World War I, and his heart was placed in St. John's Seminary's chapel.

Attending the Royal Academy on private view day, May 1932

His Eminence opens a new elementary school at Folkestone in April 1934. On the right is **Mgr. Charles Coote** (*Rector*) and the Mayor of Folkestone.

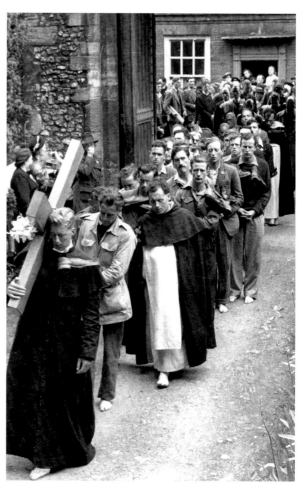

Bishop Holland of Salford visiting an archeological dig at Deansgate, Manchester in July 1978, where a remarkable fragment of earthenware linking the earliest Christian's with the city's Roman fort had just been found. The fragment, dating from about 175AD, contained a Latin palindrome (the letters read the same backwards as forwards) *Rotas opera Tenet Arepo Sator.* Whilst this translates as 'Arepo, the sower, guides the wheels with care', the words can be re-arranged to form the words *Pater Noster* (Our Father) twice, with the letters A and O (Alpha and Omega). The bishop described the coded Christian tablet as "stunning", and told *The Universe*: "If this find does not move us our hearts must be made of lead."

Barefoot priests carry the Cross through the old gateway to the Priory grounds, Walsingham, in July 1948.

With the war preventing postulants of the Little Sisters of the Poor making their novitiate at the mother house in France, a novitiate house – the first in Ireland – was opened at Clonsilia, Co. Dublin in June 1941 by the Papal Nuncio, Archbishop Robinson OFM. The picture, taken in the chapel, shows novices from Ireland, England and Scotland at the new house.

Irish Guards at Westminster Cathedral on St. Patrick's Day, 1932, when they attended High Mass in honour of the patron saint of Ireland.

Invalid passengers being loaded on to a special 'hospital' Viscount in 1971. The adapted aircraft could accomodate 35 seated passengers and 14 stretchers. At the time, Aer Lingus was the only company in the world using Viscounts for this purpose.

HRH the Prince of Wales at his special place in Westminster Cathedral during the Requiem Mass in March 1929 for **Marshal Ferdinand Foch**, supreme commander of Allied forces in World War One. Foch, a devout Catholic, was one of the most prominent French military officers in the Great War. He was the only French military commander to have been made an honorary field-marshall in the British Army.

In the ruins of the roofless nave of St. George's Cathedral, London, burnt out in an air raid, a Lourdes service was held on the vigil of the Feast of Our Lady's Assumption, in August 1943.

Ex-President **William T. Cosgrave** and his sons Michael *(left)* and Liam, photographed in the Vatican during the Irish Scout pilgrimage of 1934. Following his involvement in the 1916 Easter Rebellion Cosgrave was sentenced to death, later commuted to life imprisonment. He was, however, released a year later following his election to the British Parliament. He supported the 1921 treaty with Great Britain that set up the Irish Free State and served as President from 1922 until 1932, when he was succeeded by Éamon de Valera. He was opposition leader of his Fine Gael (United Ireland) party from 1932 until his resignation in 1944. He died in 1965. His son Liam *(pictured right)* served as Prime Minister of Ireland from 1973-77.

Sir **Roger Casement** pictured following his arrest in 1916. Prior to his involvement in the Nationalist movement Casement, who was born in Dublin in 1864, had had a distinguished diplomatic career, serving for many years as a British Consul, mainly in Africa. He was knighted for his services to the Crown in 1911 before retiring from the diplomatic service due to ill-health.

In 1913 he helped form the Irish National Volunteers. On the outbreak of war with Germany, Casement travelled to Berlin in the hope of gaining Germany's assistance in gaining Irish independence from Britain.

He was disappointed with the German response to his requests and being conviced that the planned Easter Rising wouldn't succeed, he returned to Ireland in a German submarine. Shortly after landing in Tralee, Casement was arrested by the British and charged with treason. To discredit him further a diary was produced by the British Government, alledgedly written by Casement, describing wrongdoing during his consular service in Africa.

He was found guilty of treason and hanged at Pentonville Prison, London, on 3rd August 1916, his remains being buried in the gaol.

In 1965 Casement's remains were returned to Ireland and re-interred in the family grave in Glasnevin Cemetery, Dublin. The funeral address was delivered by President Éamon de Valera, the last remaining survivor of the 1916 Easter Rising.

(Below) Draped in the Irish Tricolour, the coffin containing the remains of Sir Roger Casement is carried into Glasnevin Cemetery in 1965, followed by President de Valera.

The renowned aviator **Amy Johnson** (*centre*), caught by The *Universe* photographer with her Catholic friends **Miss Pauline Gower** (*left*) and **Miss Dorothy Spicer**, at a pub near Miss Gower's Tunbridge Wells home in May 1938.

Catholic entertainer, broadcaster and relentless charity fundraiser, **Jimmy Saville**, pictured chatting to nurses whilst doing voluntary work at the Leeds General Infirmary in April 1974.

A disused mill full of silent machinery became the temporary home of infants and juniors from St. Peter's RC School, Blackburn, while alterations were carried out to their school in July 1962. The sizing and taping room of Primrose Mill, Blackburn, which had lain derelict for more than six months after 100 years of continuous activity, was home to four classes of five to seven year olds.

The first Welsh version of the Roman Ritual made its debut on the Catholic stand at the Welsh National Eisteddfod in Barry, Glamorgan, in August 1968. The book, translated by a panel of clergy and laity, was published to coincide with the event. **Fr. John Fitzgerald, O.Carm.**, from Aberystwyth, who helped to man the stall, is pictured showing the book to some Breton visitors. During the week, Fr. Fitzgerald, a Welsh bard, also said Mass and preached in Welsh in St. Michael's Church, Barry.

Lord Russell of Killowen speaking at a garden fete he opened at the Ursuline Convent, Thornton Heath, in June 1933. From the left are Lady Russell of Killowen, Fr. Mostyn and the Mayor and Mayoress of Croydon.

Lunchtime in the Seaman's Restaurant, at Atlantic House, Liverpool, run by the Apostleship of the Sea, in October 1950.

During the great depression years of the 1930s *The Universe* organised a radical series of pilgrimages for unemployed men to Rome, culminating in a mass pilgrimage in the Holy Year of 1934. The men's places were funded by readers, with each diocese in England, Wales, Scotland and Ireland selecting a number of candidates, and every pilgrim received a small statue of Our Lady as a token of their trip. Shortly before he died, the late **Cardinal Thomas Winning** told the present editor of *The Universe* that his father had been one of those chosen from Scotland and that, shortly before he died, he gave the statue to the young Tom Winning, who had been contemplating his direction in life. The gesture convinced him to join the priesthood, and he continued to keep the little statuette in his study, praying before it every morning until his death in 2001.

Convent schoolgirls and old girls from different parts of England enjoy a reunion day at the holy wells in Walsingham Abbey in August 1937.

At the Guildford Four inquiry preliminary hearing on 4th December 1989, **Paul Hill** talks to **Sister Sarah Clarke**, from Saint Union Convent, Highgate, who, convinced of his innocence, had campaigned for 15 years to free him.

Bishop Cormac Murphy-O'Connor enjoys a chat with teenagers at the Arundel and Brighton Youth Gathering in January 1986.

Born in 1833, **Fr. Griffin**, aged 95, was the oldest priest in Ireland when *The Universe* persuaded him to step into the studio to have his photograph taken in mid-December 1928. This one of only a handful of glass plates that have survived from the early days of the newspaper. A huge and unique collection of negatives were disposed of when *The Universe* moved out of its Fleet Street premises. Prints of many still exist, but are now in a perilous state. Over the past three years technical staff at *The Universe* have been painstakingly scanning and cataloguing the collection. So far more than 3,000 images have been preserved, with an estimated 20,000 remaining.

Fr. Stephen Raynor, curate at Bethnal Green, in November 1968. Fr. Raynor made something of a literary reputation for himself that year when he published a highly popular volume of his sermons.

TV star **Derek Guyler** says hello to his first grandchild, born at St. Teresa's, Wimbledon, on 15th June 1973. Paul Joseph, who weighed in at 8lbs 6ozs on his dad's birthday, makes his debut with his mum, Judy. Before her marriage to Chris Guyler, Judy worked for *The Universe*, as had her mother Mrs. Peggy Titmuss. Derek, who played the cantankerous caretaker in the comedy series *Please, Sir*, also had a weekly showbiz column in the paper.

Archbishop Williams presenting the *Universe* shield at the Birmingham Catholic Schools Sports Association day at Cape Hill in June 1932.

A raging fire broke out at the Oratory School, Caversham, Reading, in September 1926, whilst the school was still closed for the holidays. Only three servants were in the building at the time, but they managed bravely to rescue many personal belongings, furniture and books.

Nearly 100 unidentified bodies were interred at Anfield cemetery, Liverpool, after a terrible bombing raid on the city in 1941. After a service conducted by Archbishop Downey, ARP wardens pay their final tributes to lost colleagues at the graveside.

A thousand pilgrims and holiday-makers visited Buckfast Abbey in Devon on the weekend of 23rd August 1929, to attend a special service to mark the opening of a new abbey church, which the monks had funded and built themselves. The day concluded with afternoon tea on the lawns.

An ecumenical Sea Sunday service at the dockside in Manchester in July 1979. **Fr. Arthur Keegan** (*left*), port chaplain for the Apostleship of the Sea, is joined by a choir from the St. Thomas Aquinas High School, Manchester.

The 1960 Tyburn Walk making its way through the streets of London.

Monks at Prinknash Abbey, Gloucestershire, wheeling pottery into an intermittent electric kiln in the abbey pottery in May 1963.

Cardinal Thomas Winning *(left)* was one of the Conference presidents representing eight English-speaking regions from around the world, who were posing here at the U.S. bishops headquarters in Washington on the 25th April 2000. The presidents met privately to discuss the revision of the constitution of the International Commission on English in the Liturgy. *(From left)* Cardinal Winning, U.S. Bishop Joseph A. Fiorenza, Bishop Gerald Wiesner of Canada, Archbishop Michael Bowen of England and Wales, Archbishop Wilfred F. Napier of South Africa, Cardinal Edward Bede Clancy of Australia, Bishop Peter James Cullinane of New Zealand and Irish Archbishop Sean B. Brady.

Mrs Marjorie Jackson receives her Scotwoman of the Year award fom Esther Rantzen in June 1985. Marjorie and her husband Ian, a Glasgow-based plastic surgeon, became famous after adopting David Lopez, a Peruvian boy who was abandoned as a baby in the Amazon jungle due to a disfigurement that left him without a nose, or upper jaw, and with a massive hole in the centre of his face. Rescued from a pauper's hospital in Lima by a Swiss charity worker, David was flown to Glasgow, where Ian undertook a series of groundbreaking operations to restore David's facial features. The story was eventually made into a documentary film called *The Boy David Story*.

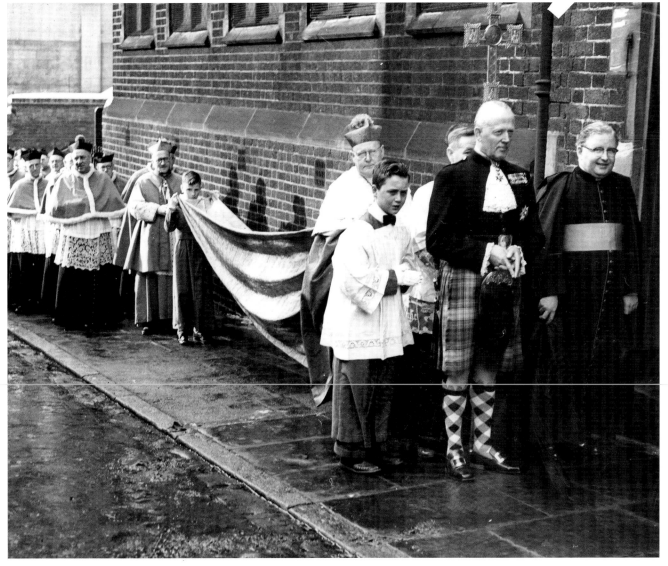

Amid the scarlet and gold robes of bishops and clergy surrounding **Dr. William Godfrey,** as he walked to his enthronment at the Pro-Cathedral of St. Nicholas in Liverpool in January 1954, was a solitary kilted figure in the green tartan of the Forbes clan. Sitting on the right of the archbishop's throne as his Gentleman-in-Attendance was the legendary aviator Lord Semphill (or Sempill). Many present recalled how, in 1933, his Lordship had flown over the site of the new cathedral in Liverpool's Brownlow Hill and dropped a wreath over the high altar as the foundation stone was being laid. Spiralling costs, and a world war, meant that the magnificent cathedral, set to rival London's St. Paul's, was never completed.

    Sir William Francis Forbes-Semphill was the 19th Baron Sempill and Baronet of Nova Scotia. He was a Royal Air Force officer and Air Ministry adviser until his retirement in 1941. An engineer, writer and airman, he was an influential propagandist for aviation at home through the Royal Aeronautical Society and abroad as the leader of technical missions to advise on the establishment of air forces. In 1932 Exeter City Council employed him to conduct an aerial survey for the best airport site, one of the first occasions that an aerial survey was utilised. He died on the 7th January 1966 in Edinburgh. His title was inherited by his eldest daughter Ann. Her son, Jamie, the 21st Lord Sempill, witnessed the abolition of the Rights of Hereditary Peers to a seat in the House of Lords, bringing to a close over 500 years of participation in the politics of Scotland and Britain.

2 EUROPEAN AIR EXPERTS HURT IN CRASH; ONE DEAD

Freak Auto Turns Over with Graf Passengers.

The Universe records that Lord Semphill was involved in a remarkable accident on the 27th October 1933, when the first Dymaxion experimental three-wheeled car was involved in a fatal accident just outside the grounds of the Century of Progress World's Fair in Chicago. The American driver of the car, Francis T. Turner, was a famous racing driver, employed by the Gulf Refining Company, that had purchased the car. The two passengers in the car, Lord Semphill and Charles Dollfuss of Paris, were seriously injured. Forbes-Sempill and Dollfuss had arrived at the World's Fair on the Graf Zeppelin, and were being rushed to the airport to catch a plane to Akron, Ohio where they would meet the Zeppelin for its return trip from New York to Europe. Lord Semphill, who was sitting beside the driver, hurt his head very badly, and was in the hospital in Chicago in a very critical condition for a number of days, during which time he received a private phone call from his close friend, King George V.

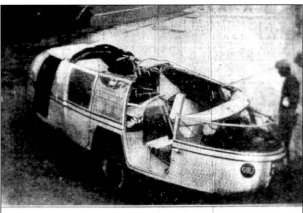

[TRIBUNE Photo.]

EXPERIMENTAL THREE WHEELED AUTO OVERTURNS, 1 KILLED, 2 HURT
Wreckage of three wheeled Dymaxion auto after accident yesterday on the... Francis T. Turner, driver, was killed, and those injured were two passengers on the... Zeppelin: Charles Dollfus of France and the Hon. W. F. Forbes-Sempill.

(Dominic) Bevan Wyndham-Lewis FRSL (9th March 1891– 21st November 1969) was a British writer best known for his humorous contributions to newspapers and for biographies. His family were originally from Wales, but he was born in Liverpool and brought up in Cardiff.

He served in the Welch Regiment during World War I, and afterwards joined the *Daily Express* where he was briefly Literary Editor.

In 1919 he was put in charge of the paper's humorous 'By the Way' column and adopted the pen name Beachcomber. However he was not happy confining his contribution to humour, and gave up the column to the better-known J. B. Morton.

He lived in Paris from the mid 1920s while doing historical research (although he contributed a column called 'At the Sign of the Blue Moon' to the *Daily Mail* which his followers regard as his most outstanding body of humorous work).

In 1928 he wrote a biography of François Villon, a roguish poet from the 15th century. Later biographies of Kings Louis XI and Charles V appeared.

Perhaps his best-remembered work is as an editor, not as a writer: *The Stuffed Owl* which he co-edited with Charles Lee. This anthology of 'bad verse' is justly famous as one of the funniest of all poetry collections, featuring William Wordsworth, Edgar Allan Poe and many others at considerably less than their best.

Wyndham-Lewis converted to the Catholic faith in 1921. Later in the 1930s, after returning to Britain, he turned to humorous anthologies, and in 1954 he collaborated with Ronald Searle on *The Terror of St Trinian's* (under the pen-name Timothy Shy).

Later work also included biographies of Boswell, Ronsard, Molière, Francisco Goya and Miguel de Cervantes.

He also co-wrote, with Charles Bennett, the screenplay for the first version of Alfred Hitchcock's *The Man Who Knew Too Much* (1934).

Machester United manager **Matt Busby** (later Sir) pulls a pint for Canon John Murphy at the opening of the new Langley Men's Club in Middleton, Manchester, on the 17th May 1963.

Canon John Francis Murphy was something of a legend in the Diocese of Salford. He was sent to Langley in 1953 by his former parish priest, the late Bishop Marshall of Salford, with £1,000 from the bishop to establish a Mass centre there.

His first 'church' was a council house, with Mass being said in the tiny sitting room. Soon after, Canon Murphy managed to secure the use of a workmen's canteen at a building site for Sunday Mass.

Early in 1954 a corrugated hut was bought, which served as a temporary church until 1957 when the parish had grown to 6,000. At this point Canon Murphy opened another church,

St. Columba's, at the other end of the estate, and this served its purpose until a permanent new church was built in 1961. Speaking at the opening of St. Mary's, Bishop Beck of Salford commented that the congregation had been drawn into the area from 38 parishes, and local schools were having to make special arrangements to cope with 2,000 new children in the area.

Sir Alexander Matthew "Matt" Busby, CBE (26th May 1909 – 20th January 1994) was a Scottish football player, most noted for managing Manchester United between 1945 – 1969 and again for the 1970-1971 season. He was born in a two-roomed pitman's cottage in the mining village of Orbiston (now part of Bellshill), North Lanarkshire, of Lithuanian ancestry and was raised a practising Roman Catholic.

Few visitors to Westminster Cathedral today will know that another (non-Catholic) church once stood alongside it on the famous piazza, nor that the cathedral itself came so close to destruction.

Following a visit from the Luftwaffe in May 1945, **Cardinal Griffin** addressed Massgoers at the cathedral, saying: "We must here express our deep gratitude to Almighty God that our beautiful cathedral has been spared and we thank all those who have so generously offered their prayers for its protection."

A second bomb exploded in the roadway at the side of the cathedral, and a third made a huge crater in the cathedral grounds.

Bishop Robert Dobson takes to the scales at a parish fete in Liverpool in July 1928. Robert Dobson (1867–1942) was born in New Orleans and became a priest in 1891. He was appointed Auxiliary Bishop of Liverpool on the 22nd August 1922, and Titular Bishop of Cynopolis in Arcadia in November of the same year. He died in office on the 6th January 1942, aged 75.

In May 1928, **Archishop McIntyre of Birmingham** emerges from the city's St. Chad's cathedral after celebrating pontifical High Mass in the morning, "attended by the Magistrati in Master Melvin and Mr Frank Wain," said *The Universe*. Standing immediately behind the archbishop (wearing a papal sash over his waistcoat) is the Birmingham entrepreneur **Sir Martin John Melvin**, (1879-1952) who owned *The Universe* Catholic weekly at this time. Sir Martin's father left Ireland around 1845 and sold rabbitskins in

Birmingham Bullring. He made his first fortune salvaging a sunken cargo ship. His son followed in his entrepreneurial footsteps, becoming the owner of a successful number of businesses in the Birmingham area, before becoming Chairman of Associated Catholic Newspapers, and hence owner of *The Universe*, in 1917.

He organised several *Universe* pilgrimages for the unemployed to Rome in the 1930s, even striking a commemorative medal for the pilgrims.

Unfortunately things didn't go too well for the archbishop later in the day, when according to *The Universe* reporter, the horses for the carriage to carry him around the city became "restive" and a group of young Catholic men were 'volunteered' to replace them!

Marist nuns from England try their hand at tank driving during a break in a visit to Germany in October 1965. The nuns made an annual trip to do catechetical work among the children of members of the U.S. Forces based in the Rhineland.

Polish pilots kneel in a hangar "somewhere in England" during Mass, celebrated by their Polish chaplain in November 1941.

A remarkable moment in English Catholic history, captured by a *Universe* photographer on 19th August 1934. **Cardinal Bourne** (riding in car) and the English bishops lead 3,000 pilgrims in procession to honour Our Lady of Walsingham, at Walsingham, Norfolk, in the first Catholic procession in this holy spot since the Reformation. A request to Lady Gurney, who owned the grounds, for permission for the pilgrimage to enter the priory grounds, was refused, according the *Universe* report of the event. The pilgrims attended Pontifical High Mass in the church of St. John the Baptist at Norwich, and afterwards went to the Slipper Chapel where an open air altar had been built on the banks of the Stiffkey. The Sacrament was carried by the Bishop of Northampton.

In the workshop at Quarr Abbey a monk is pictured at the engineer's bench in November 1954, using what the *Universe* described as "modern electrical lathes and oxy-acetylene burners" for welding.

Archbishop Keating of Liverpool *(by stone)* with **Bishop Pearson of Lancaster** and the Mayor of Wigan, Councillor J. McCurdy, wearing his chain of office, after Mgr. Pearson laid the foundation stone for a new wing at St. Joseph's College, Upholland, in October 1926. The new wing formed accommodation for the superior and teaching staff at the seminary.

The scene in All Saints Street, Hastings, Sussex, on Sunday the 30th July 1960, during the town's annual pilgrimage from the church of St. Mary, Star of the Sea, to the ancient shrine of Our Lady in the ruins of Hastings Castle.

The Earl of Dumfries, **John Crichton-Stuart**, 5th Marquess of Bute (4th August 1907 – 14th August 1956), and **Lady Eileen Forbes**, daughter of Bernard Forbes, 8th Earl of Granard, pictured making their marriage vows at Clonguish, Newtown Forbes, Co. Longford, on the 26th April 1932.

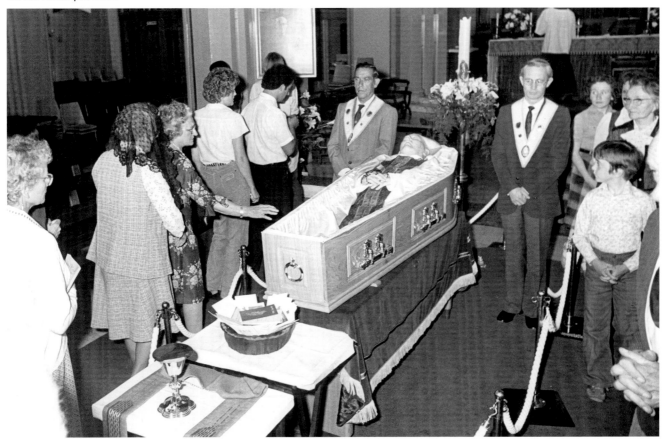

The people of the Nottingham diocese pay their final respects to **Monsignor Edward Ellis**, their bishop from 1944 to 1974, during his lying-in-state at St. Barnabus's Cathedral in July 1979. He is being guarded by representatives of the Knights of St. Columba.

In 1944 the *Universe* photographer travelled across the UK in search of pictures showing how Catholics were coping with the difficult conditions. Although this particular image doesn't exactly illustrate wartime difficulties, he obviously couldn't resist capturing this shot of a Cistercian brother visiting a sick companion at the Mount St. Bernard Abbey in Leicestershire's Charnwood Forest. It seems that, to enable a sick brother to live in the open air, the monks built him a thatched chalet near the main church door where, on doctor's orders, the monk slept throughout the year. The "home" contained a bed, a crucifix, and a sacred picture, the brother's sole posessions.

English and Palestinian Scouts meet up in Rome after a visit to St. Peter's in September 1925.

Part of the crowd of 400,000 Catholics at Thingwall Park, Liverpool, for the 1929 Catholic Emancipation Celebrations.

BERNARD MARMADUKE FITZALAN-HOWARD

16TH DUKE OF NORFOLK, KG, GCVO, GBE, TD, PC

MAY 30TH 1908-JANUARY 31ST 1975

The 16th Duke in full regalia *(second left)* officiates for the first time at the opening of the new Parliamentary session, November 1930.

Bernard Marmaduke Fitzalan-Howard, 16th Duke of Norfolk, KG, GCVO, GBE, TD, PC (May 30th 1908-January 31st 1975), was the eldest surviving son of Henry Fitzalan-Howard, 15th Duke of Norfolk, who died when Bernard was only 9 years old.

He was educated at The Oratory School and was commissioned into the Royal Horse Guards in 1931, but resigned his commission in 1933. He joined the 4th (Territorial Army) Battalion, Royal Sussex Regiment in 1934, and was promoted Major in 1939.

He served in World War II, where he was wounded in action.

The position of Earl Marshal is one of the Great Offices of State, The Marshal has the responsibility of organising coronations, state funerals and the monarch's coronation, and along with the Lord Great Chamberlain also officiate sat the State Opening of Parliament.

His seniority gives him precedence after the Lord Great Chamberlain and before all peers of his own degree other than Royal dukes.

Since the sixteenth century, the Earl Marshal has also had authority over the kings of arms, heralds and pursuivants at the College of Arms, the body concerned with heraldry, and the his warrant has to be obtained before a grant of arms can be made.

The office of Earl Marshal is an hereditary position always occupied by the Catholic Dukes of Norfolk. The post originates from the office of Marshal, one of the King's chief military officers during the Middle Ages. At that time he also became responsible for coronations and other State ceremonies. In the middle of the fourteenth century, the Marshal became one of the two joint judges of the Court of Chivalry.

In 1386 the title changed from Marshal to Earl Marshal, which has been used ever since.

Many of the Marshals from the twelfth century onwards were related to each other, but the office was not originally hereditary. The role only became hereditary in 1672, when Henry Howard, who succeeded to the dukedom of Norfolk in 1677, was appointed hereditary Earl Marshal.

The Duke and Duchess of Norfolk attend the Vatican in 1970 for the canonisation of the 40 English Martyrs.

HM The Queen is escorted along the corridors of the vatican to the Papal appartments on her visit to Pope John XXIII
on the 5th May 1961. The Queen wears black lace as only female Catholic monarchs have the right "privilege du blanc"
to wear white when meeting the Holy Father.

The Catholic writer **Hilaire Belloc** was guest speaker at this *Universe* luncheon held in London in February 1934.

Cardinal Bourne takes afternoon tea during a visit to St. Edmund's College, Ware, in June 1934.

It looks as though TV personality **Peter Moloney** is doing his charity walk in easy style, but it was mainly for the benefit of the *Universe* photographer that he took to this pram in May 1968. He and Fr. George Giarchi, C.S.S.R *(pushing the pram)* led 100 youngsters from the Catholic youth centre, Blackburn, on a 38 mile sponsored walk to Lancaster to raise funds for the Bethany hostel for girls, Blackburn.

Admirers of the Catholic writer G.K. Chesterton will be shocked by this story, which appeared in *The Universe* in August 1969.

Fr. Kevin Scannell, parish priest of St. Walburga's, Shipley, Yorks, told *The Universe* that he had decided to bequeath his priceless collection of books and manuscripts of G.K. Chesterton to Canada because of what he described as "a lack of interest in the famous writer in this country".

The 67 year-old priest said that "no one in Britain seems to appreciate that Chesterton was a great theological and philosphical writer and a brilliant Catholic thinker. It's different on the other side of the Atlantic, so I shall bequeath my collection to the Pontifical Institute of Medieval Studies in Toronto."

Fr. Scammell's collection of Chestertonia was the largest in the world, and included all the material that had been given to him by Chesterton's secretary, Miss Dorothy Collins – manuscripts, photographs, sketches, and numerous signed first editions!

Manchester United manager **Tommy Docherty** did a transfer deal of a different kind in January 1975 when he gave away his daughter Catherine at Holy Angels, Hale Barns, Cheshire.

LEEDS GIRL CURED

The Catholics of Leeds and district made a public act of thanksgiving on Sunday the 12th June 1927, for the reported cure of **Miss Mary Healy**, a member of St. Francis' congregation, Hotheck, who took part in a pilgrimage organised by the Society of Our Lady of Lourdes.

For nearly four years, up to the time she reached Lourdes, Miss Healy, who was 22 at the time, had been unable to walk without crutches owing to a tubercular ankle. After her pilgrimage she became able to walk unaided, and her crutches were left behind in the Lourdes grotto. It is stated that four doctors, including one non-Catholic, who examined her on her arrival, afterwards declared that she had been cured. Since an injury nearly four years previously, Miss Healy had been under constant medical care, and, after treatment at the Leeds General Infirmary, had spent six months In Killirgbeck Sanatorium. When she left doctors told her mother they did not think she would ever get well again.

Miss Healy is pictured being congratulated by her parish priest, Canon McAuliffe, just before she took part in the celebrations.

Miss Mary Kellett travelled to Lourdes an invalid on a stretcher in August 1932 with the annual Salford Pilgrimage, but returned with the use of her limbs. Miss Kellet is pictured *(top)* being greeted by her father at Chorley railway station, and both were met by huge crowds outside *(above)*.

When Mrs. Joan Matthewman of Mill Hill, Blackburn, Lancs., *(right)* was expecting her third child, she discovered that she had cancer of the shoulder, and doctors advised an abortion.

Mrs. Matthewman refused and, after the child's birth, the cancer became worse. Later she had a fourth child. Then, following a Novena to the Forty Martyrs, she made a complete recovery.

She eventually died on the 8th March 1963, of a chronic abcess in the right mastoid. Her doctors conducted a rigorous post-mortem examination but found no trace of the cancer of the shoulder. The Sacred Congregation for the Causes of Saints accepted the cure as miraculous.

SHEILA
KAYE-SMITH

CATHOLIC AUTHOR
WHO BROUGHT
THE MASS TO
RURAL SUSSEX

(Left) Sheila
pictured in
October, 1929,
at the time of
her conversion,
which made front
page news in
The Universe of
25th October.

Sheila Kaye-Smith (4th February 1887 – 14th January 1956) was an English Catholic writer, known for her many novels set in the borderlands of Sussex and Kent in the English regional tradition. Her 1923 book *The End of the House of Alard* became a best-seller, and gave her prominence; it was followed by other successes and her books enjoyed world-wide sales.

The daughter of a doctor, Sheila was born in St Leonards-on-Sea, near Hastings, in Sussex, where she lived most of her life. In 1924 she married the Rev. Theodore Penrose Fry, an Anglican clergyman, and in 1925 wrote a book on Anglo-Catholicism. They were both received into the Catholic Church on Monday the 21st October 1929 by the preacher Fr. C.C. Martindale at the Church of the Immaculate Conception, Farm Street, London.

They moved to Northiam in Sussex, where they lived at Little Doucegrove, a large converted oast house. Soon afterwards, having noted their own and some of their neighbours' need for a nearby Catholic church, they bought land on which they established a Catholic chapel, St Teresa of Lisieux, at Northiam, which still enjoys a large congregation. Sheila is buried in the churchyard there.

Kaye-Smith's fiction was noted for being rooted in rural concerns: the 19th century agricultural depression, farming, legacies, land rents, strikes, the changing position of women and the effects of industrialisation on the countryside and provincial life. Her descriptions of the Sussex countryside, coast and marsh are still regarded as some of the finest. She also produced many short stories, and had articles published in national journals, magazines and newspapers, including *The Universe*.

Arguably her most famous novel, *Joanna Godden* was based in Romney Marsh and filmed in 1947 as *The Loves of Joanna Godden* starring Googie Withers and with a score by Ralph Vaughan Williams.

The Universe described her as: "a favourite speaker on Anglo-Catholic platforms, where her brilliant addresses, coupled with her quiet earnestness and avoidance of the controversial manner have proved deeply impressive. Since for her the beat of life has always been strong in the fields she knows, and since for her Christianity is vital and ever-present, she speaks of Christ walking in the roads about her home, as the Irish peasants do. She understood in this the reality of religion and the truth of the Sacraments, and has been in her poetry and in her novels an exponent of the movement towards Catholicism in the Anglican Church."

(*Above*) June 1934, and Sheila calls at isolated hamlets and farms in the northern districts of Sussex to bring Catholics to Mass.
(*Below*) Relaxing at home with husband T. Penrose Fry, and Fr. Windham, the Southwark Travelling Missioner who acted as Sheila's chauffeur on their Mass visits around the county.

The historic visit of **Pope John Paul II** to Scotland began on the 31st May 1982 as the Holy Father kissed the ground on his arrival at RAF Turnhouse, near Edinburgh, watched by **Cardinal Gordon Gray**, Archbishop of St. Andrews and Edinburgh *(above)*. He then went to Murrayfield Stadium for the Scottish National Youth Pilgrimage where more than 40,000 young people applauded his speech and sang *You'll Never Walk Alone*. On the 1st June he met the Moderator of the General Assembly of the Church of Scotland and other Church leaders in Edinburgh. Afterwards he toured the wards of St Joseph's Hospital for the Severely Handicapped, near Edinburgh. Finally, he joined the Most Rev. Thomas Winning, Archbishop of Glasgow, and 300,000 people from across the country for a national Mass in Glasgow's Bellahouston Park, after which the crowd sang *Will Ye No Come Back Again?* The momentous visit concluded with an informal farewell and words of gratitude from Bishop Conti of Aberdeen.

The Pope in his popemobile at the Murrayfield Stadium, where he was greeted by 40,000 youngsters.

Open air Mass at Bellahousten Park.

A fond farewell from **Bishop Mario Conti** of Aberdeen.

SIMON ELWES

JUNE 29TH 1902-
AUGUST 6TH 1975

Simon Edmund Vincent Paul Elwes (June 29th 1902-August 6th 1975) was an English society portrait painter and scion to the Cary-Elwes recusant family (originally known as the "Cary-Elwes" family, but now many branches of the family are known simply as "Elwes") which includes noted British monks and bishops, such as Abbott Columba Cary-Elwes, Archbishop Dudley Cary-Elwes and Father Luke Cary-Elwes.

Elwes (pronounced "El-wez") was born on 29th June, 1902 at Hothorpe Hall, Northamptonshire, the sixth and youngest son (two daughters were born later) of Gervase Cary Elwes (1866-1921), diplomat and tenor who was killed in a railway accident while on American tour, and his wife, Lady Winifride Mary Elizabeth Feilding, daughter of Rudolph William Basil Feilding, 8th Earl of Denbigh and 7th Earl of Desmond (1823-1892).

Elwes attended two Catholic schools, Lady Cross School, Seaford, and The Oratory, Edgbaston. In 1918, at the age of sixteen, he entered the Slade School of Fine Art.

After leaving the Slade he spent the next eight years in Paris. In 1926, Elwes returned to England and married the Hon. Gloria Elinor Rodd, the daughter of Rennell Rodd, 1st Baron Rennell, diplomat and scholar. They had four sons, one of whom died in infancy, including portrait painter Dominick Elwes, who became a cause célèbre in 1957 when he eloped with shipping heiress, Tessa Kennedy.

The following year Elwes showed a portrait at the Royal Academy of Arts of

May 1938 Simon Elwes pictured with his portrait of Queen Mary which was exhibited in that years Royal Academy.

Lady Lettice Lygon. She was the first of his many noble
sitters that would include many of Britain's Royal Family. Thereafter, his portraits hung in the summer exhibition of the Royal Academy every year. In London's Mayfair and on Manhattan's Park Avenue he established
himself as a stylish portraitist.

He was created a Knight of Malta in 1929 and four years later was elected a member of the Royal Society of Portrait Painters.

At the outbreak of World War II, Elwes joined the Welsh Guards, to be transferred later to the 10th Royal Hussars in Egypt serving as a Lieutenant Colonel.

After fighting in the battles of Benghazi, Mersa Matruh, and Knightsbridge, he was made an official war artist. In Cairo he painted King Farouk, Queen Farida and

Henry Maitland Wilson, General Officer Commanding (GOC) British Troops in Egypt.

In South Africa he painted portraits of King Paul I of the Hellenes and his wife the Queen consort of Greece, Frederica of Hanover as well as Prime Minister, J. C. Smuts.

In India he painted the Viceroy, Archibald Wavell, the Maharaja of Patiala, Lord Louis Mountbatten (later Earl Mountbatten of Burma), and Indian Army soldiers who had won the Victoria Cross.

Returning to England after the war, Elwes suffered a near-death stroke at the age of 43. He spent two years in hospital but was never able to use his right hand for painting again. As soon as he could stand, though, Elwes taught himself to paint with his left.

He surmounted his disability enough to become president of the Guild of Catholic Artists, vice-president of the Royal Society of Portrait Painters from 1953, an associate of the Royal Academy in 1956, and a full RA in 1967.

One observer who witnessed Elwes at a meeting of the Royal Academy in his later years, recalls: "Handsome, fresh of complexion, finely dressed, with a scarlet flower in his buttonhole, he enriched the proceedings with his smile, no less than with his air of being a visitor from a world more carefree and elegant than the one in which deficits and disappointments were certain to be discussed."

In the last months of his life, Elwes had to be pushed about in a wheelchair, hardly able to speak.

He died on the 6th August, 1975, in Sussex. His son, Dominick, died in the same year, as did his wife, Gloria, who died two months later.

Lady Winefride Elwes (nee Feilding, daughter of the 8th Earl of Denbigh) Simon Elwes' mother.

In January 1931 world famous aviatrix, the Hull born, Amy Johnson (July 1st 1903-January 5th 1941) crashed her plane at Krasnosieice in Poland. She was unhurt and given shelter by the parish priest, Fr. Serejke, with whom she is pictured here.

Snatching a brief spell during hard fighting on the Cherbourg Peninsula in July 1944, Allied soldiers hear Mass celebrated by their chaplain in the cover of trees just behind the front line. *The Universe* pointed out that "most of the Catholics in the British Army made their Confession and received Holy Communion before setting out to liberate occupied France."

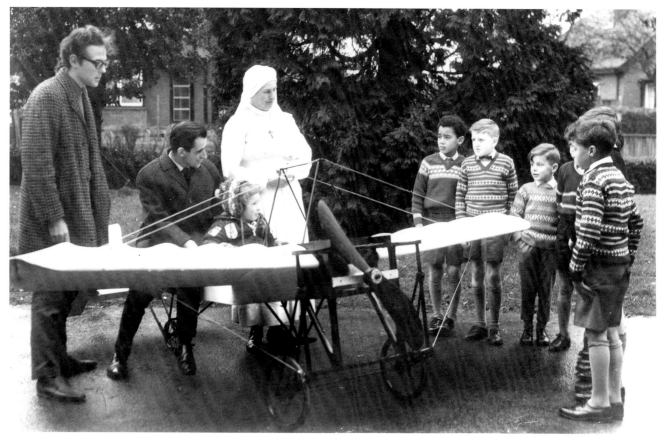

"Contact, chocks away!" **Mother Teresa** with some of her young charges at the Fr. Hudson Homes in Coleshill, near Birmingham watch as an intrepid six year old prepares to test a Bleriot model aeroplane. Also pictured are two members of the Tudor Falcon Model Aero Club, of Sutton Coldfield, who made and presented the machine to the Home. It boasted a 10ft wingspan and the *Universe* reported that "it will taxi quite well – if the groundcrew are prepared to push!" The model was an exact replica of the Bleriot XI monoplane which flew the English Channel in 1909.

Monsignor William Shepherd, former Vicar General for the Navy and later parish priest of Our Lady, St. Maws, Cornwall, leaves Buckingham Palace with his sisters in March 1957 after receiving the CBE.

At an ARP post "somewhere in the Home Counties" in October 1939 a nun hands a welcome cup of tea to an air raid warden.

When disc jockey **Jimmy Savile** was in Fort William in August 1973 to take the role of Chieftain at the Lochaber Highland Games, he took time off for a very special occasion. **Fr. Denis O'Connell**, of St. Patrick's, Kilsyth, was joined by two deacons from the Kiltegan Fathers in a Mass for Mrs. Agnes Savile ('The Duchess'), Jimmy's beloved mother, who had died the previous year. Jimmy is pictured chatting after the service to Fr. O'Connell (left), Fr. Morrison, parish priest of Coal, and the two (un-named) deacons.

In September 1938, a Franciscan priest announced the idea of a badge to be worn by Catholics in wartime – particularly for use with gas masks.

Fr. Anthony O.S.F.C., of Erith, Kent, also designed a badge to be worn by clergy.

The first style was printed on rubber with an adhesive backing for fixing to the gas mask *(top right)*, and for clergy there were two types – a pin brooch, or attached to a wrist strap *(below right)*.

They were sold on a non-profit basis, with reduced prices for quantities order from clergy, repositories and traders.

Cardinal Hinsley gave the idea his approval, and chose the final design.

The A.R.P. department of the Home Office agreed that it was important to identify Catholics by this means in wartime.

Agreements for the manufacture and distribution of the badges were reached with Liturgicarft Limited, of 18 Grape Street, London WC2.

Blacksmith Carthusians working in their forge at the monastery at Cowfold, in Sussex in March 1929. Although they led strenuous lives, the monks of Cowfold were noted for their longevity. According to *The Universe*, experts from the Ministry of Health had even visited the monastery to study their mode of living and try to discover the secret of their immunity from sickness.

Three men on their way to work in October pause to look at an inscribed, three foot circular slab of Portland Stone after it had been placed on a road island at the junction of the Edgeware and Bayswater roads at Marble Arch, London, to commemorate the site of the ancient Tyburn tree gallows, where so many of the martyrs suffered a cruel death. Tyburn is the most blood-saturated spot in London, where thousands of executions took place from the 12th century – and perhaps earlier – up to 1783.

Lord Pakenham, Minister responsible for British affairs in Germany, with his wife and family in January 1948 when their eighth child was baptised at St. Edward the Confessor's church, Golders Green, London. The new baby was a boy and was named Kevin.

Francis Aungier Pakenham, 7th Earl of Longford, KG, PC (5th December 1905 – 3rd August 2001) was a politician, author, and social reformer. During the immediate post-war food crisis in Germany, Lord Longford was appointed Minister for the British zones in Germany and Austria. Asked about his concerns for the German people, he said famously: "Take it from me that the

German food crisis is my first concern when I say my prayers in the morning and when I go to bed at night."

At 25 he joined the Conservative Party but his future wife, Elizabeth, who he had met at Oxford, persuaded him to become a socialist and convert to Roman Catholicism from Protestantism.

An active social worker, he was chairman of the National Society for Physically Handicapped Children, chairman of Mencap and of the National Youth Employment Council. He also presided over various inquiries relating to crime and punishment and the re-habilitation of ex-prisoners.

Miss Una O'Connor, *(above)* noted Catholic film and stage star, was the adjudicator when the contests of the Catholic Drama League Festival took place in London in May 1939. Pictured with Miss O'Connor are Bishop Myers and Mr. Neil Muldoon, Chairman of the League.

Una O'Connor (23rd October 1880 – 4th February 1959) was an Irish actress who worked extensively in theatre before becoming a notable character actress in film.

Born Agnes Teresa McGlade to a Catholic nationalist family in Belfast, and educated at St. Vincent's National School, she changed her name when she began her acting career with Dublin's Abbey Theatre.

For many years, she worked in Ireland and England as a stage actress, for example in *The Starlight Express* at the Kingsway Theatre in London (1915-1916). She appeared in Alfred Hitchcock's *Murder!* (1930).

Despite her lengthy apprenticeship she had not attracted much attention until she was chosen by Noel Coward to appear in *Cavalcade* (1933). Her success led her to Hollywood to reprise her role and, with its success, O'Connor decided to remain there.

A favourite of the director James Whale, among her most successful and best remembered roles are her performances in Whale's *The Invisible Man* (1933), in which she played the hysterical innkeeper *(right)*, and *Bride of Frankenstein* (1935).

O'Connor also appeared in supporting roles in various theatre productions, and achieved an outstanding success in the role of Janet McKenzie, the nearly deaf housemaid, in Agatha Christie's *Witness for the Prosecution* at Henry Miller's Theatre on Broadway from 1954 until 1956. As one of the witnesses, in what was essentially a serious drama, O'Connor's character was intended to provide comic relief, as so many of her past characterisations had.

O'Connor was highly praised for her work, and also played the role in the highly successful Billy Wilder film version of the same name in 1957. It was her final film performance. By this time she was in her late 70s, and decided to retire. She died, never having married, in New York City from heart disease, aged 78.

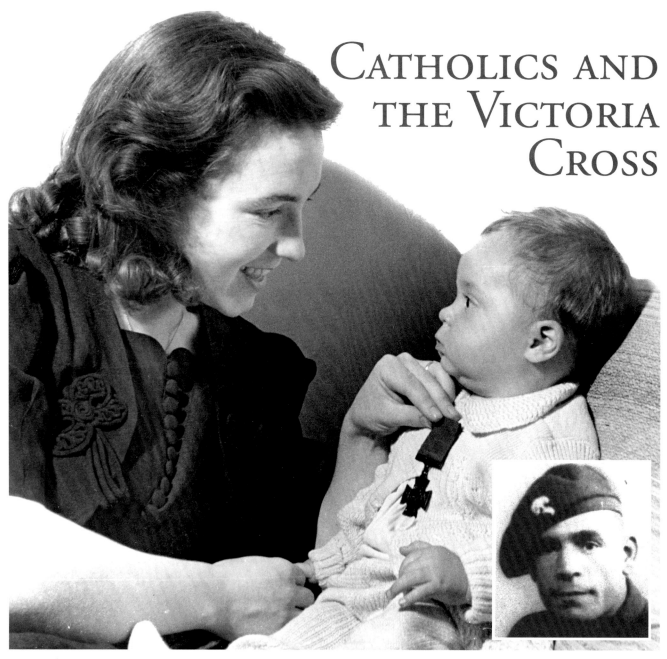

CATHOLICS AND THE VICTORIA CROSS

Lance Corporal **Harry Nicholls** was the first person to be awarded the Victoria Cross in World War II (though not the earliest action to be recognised). Born in Nottingham, he was serving as a Lance-Corporal with the 3rd Battalion of the Grenadier Guards when he performed the deeds for which he was awarded the VC.

From his citation: "On the 21st May, 1940, Lance-Corporal Nicholls was commanding a section in the right forward platoon of his company when the company was ordered to counter-attack. At the very start of the advance he was wounded in the arm by shrapnel but continued to lead his section forward, as the company came over a small ridge, the enemy opened heavy machine-gun fire at close range.

"Lance-Corporal Nicholls, realising the danger to his company, immediately seized a Bren Gun and dashed forward towards the machine guns, firing from the hip. He succeeded in silencing first one machine gun then two other machine guns, in spite of being again severely wounded.

"Lance-Corporal Nicholls then went up to a higher piece of ground and engaged the German infantry massed behind, causing many casualties and continued to fire until he had no more ammunition left. He was wounded at least four times in all but absolutely refused to give in. There is no doubt that his gallant action was instrumental in enabling the company to reach its objective and in causing the enemy to fall back across the River Scheldt. Lance-Corporal Nicholls has since been reported to have been killed in action."

In August 1940 his widow took their eight month old daughter Carol to Buckingham Palace with Lance-Corporal Nicholls' parents, where they were received privately by His Majesty The King, who consoled them, and then placed Nicolls' medal on baby Carol's smock. The poignant meeting made national news, and the story and picture (above) appeared on the front page of The Universe on the 9th August 1940.

But, remarkably, the last sentence of the citation was incorrect; the following month news was received via the Red Cross that Nicholls had been captured by the Germans and taken to Stalag XBB, where he spent the rest of the war. After receiving this wonderful news Mrs. Nicholls returned the medal to the King, saying that her husband would be back to collect it himself – which he did, in June 1945.

Sadly, after the war Nicholls was beset by health problems arising from his serious wounds, and he died prematurely in Leeds on the 10th September 1975. His medals are in the Grenadier Guards RHQ, Wellington Barracks, London.

Dennis Donnini (17th November 1925 –18th January 1945) was born of Italian origin, and attended Corby Grammar School in Sunderland, now St. Aidans School. His Father was Italian and owned an ice cream palour. Dennis was a parishioner at Our Lady of the Assumption, Easington Colliery.

He was 19 years old, and a Fusilier in the 4/5th Battalion, The Royal Scots Fusiliers, British Army during the Second World War when the deed took place for which he was awarded the VC.

On the 18th January 1945 during Operation Blackcock, Fusilier Donnini's platoon was ordered to attack the small village of Stein in Germany, close to the Dutch border. On leaving their trench they immediately came under heavy fire from a house and the fusilier was hit in the head.

After recovering consciousness he charged 30 yards down the open road and hurled a grenade through the nearest window, whereupon the enemy fled, pursued by Fusilier Donnini and the survivors of his platoon.

He was wounded a second time, but continued firing his Bren gun until he was killed after the grenade he was carrying was hit by a bullet and exploded.

His gallantry had enabled his comrades to overcome twice their own number of the enemy.

On the 20th July 1945 *The Universe* accompanied Fusilier Donnini's A.T.S. sister, Silvia, and his father, Mr. Alfredo Donnini, 65, *(right)* to Buckingham Palace to collect his VC from the King. Another A.T.S. sister, Corrina. waited outside.

The King commented on the Donnini family war record: two sons killed, another a prisoner for five years, and two daughters in the ATS.

Fusilier Donnini is buried in the Sittard War Cemetery, Limburg, and his medal is on display at the Easington Colliery Working men's Club, Seaside Lane, Easington Colliery, Co. Durham.

19 YEAR OLD SAVED HIS PALS

SELFLESS ACTS OF COURAGE

Paul Triquet, VC, CD (2nd April, 1910 – 8th August, 1980) was a Canadian recipient of the Victoria Cross *(pictured top right)*. At the time he was 33 years old, and a Captain in the Royal 22e Régiment, Canadian Army.

On the 14th December 1943 during the attack on Casa Berardi, Italy, when all the other officers and half the men of his company had been killed or wounded, Captain Triquet dashed forward with the remaining men and broke through the enemy resistance. He then forced his way on with his small force – now reduced to two sergeants and 15 men – into a position on the outskirts of Casa Berardi.

They held out against attacks from overwhelming numbers until the remainder of the battalion relieved them the next day. Throughout the action Captain Triquet's utter disregard for danger and his cheerful encouragement were an inspiration to his men.

Triquet later achieved the rank of Brigadier General. His memorial plaque is at Mount Royal Crematorium, Quebec City, Quebec, Canada. (Ashes interred in the Royal 22nd Regimental Memorial, The Citadel, Quebec). His medals can be seen at the Citadelle de Quebec.

Rear Admiral Sir **Anthony Cecil Capel Miers** VC, KBE, CB, DSO & Bar (11th November 1906 – 30th June 1985) was a Scottish recipient of the Victoria Cross *(centre right)*. He was 35 years old, and a commander in the Royal Navy during the Second World War when the deed took place for which he was awarded the VC.

On the 4th March 1942 in Corfu Harbour, north-western Greece, Commander Miers, commanding HM Submarine *Torbay,* having followed an enemy convoy into the harbour the previous day, fired torpedoes at a destroyer and two 5,000-ton transports, scoring hits on the two supply ships, which almost certainly sank. *Torbay* then had a very hazardous withdrawal to the open sea, enduring 40 depth-charges. The submarine had been in closely patrolled enemy waters for 17 hours.

Later Sir Anthony, he achieved in 1956 the rank of Rear Admiral. He is Buried at Tomnahurich Cemetery, Inverness, Scotland, and his Victoria Cross is displayed at the Imperial War Museum, London.

Edward Stephen Fogarty Fegen VC SGM *(bottom right)* was born in Southsea, Hampshire on 8th October 1891, and recorded as 'missing (presumed dead)' in the Atlantic Ocean on 5th November 1940. He was 49 years old, and an Acting Captain in the Royal Navy.

On the 5th November 1940 in the Atlantic, Captain Fegen, commanding the armed merchantman *HMS Jervis Bay,* was escorting 37 ships of Convoy HX-84, when they were attacked by the German pocket battleship *Admiral Scheer.* Captain Fegen immediately engaged the enemy head-on, thus giving the ships of the convoy time to scatter.

Out-gunned and on fire *Jervis Bay* maintained the unequal fight for three hours, although the captain's right arm was shattered and his bridge was shot from under him. He went down with his ship but it was due to him that 31 ships of the convoy escaped.

Agnellus Matthew Andrew, Catholic bishop and broadcaster, was born near Glasgow in 1908. He was ordained in 1932, and became assistant to the head of religious broadcasting at the BBC from 1955 to 1967, and adviser to the Independent Broadcasting Authority from 1968 to 1975. He became well known as a TV commentator for many papal and national events, and was founder and director of the National Catholic Radio and TV Centre at Hatch End, Greater London from 1955 to 1980. On the 25th February 1980 Pope John Paul II, having elevated the Rev. Agnellus Andrew O.F.M. to the titular Bishopric of Numa, nominated the new bishop as Vice-President of the Pontifical Commission for Social Communications, to work alongside Bishop Deskur, the President, who had suffered a stroke in October 1978 and was in poor health. Bishop Andrew, who had been President of UNDA (Association Catholique Internationale pour la Radio et la Télévision), placed his vast knowledge of the problems inherent in social communications at the service of the Commission. He retired from the post on the 16th July 1983, but remained Vice President Emeritus until his death on the 19th January 1987, aged 78. He is remembered in the annual Andrew Cross awards for religious journalism.

PADRE WHO GAVE HOPE TO NORTH KOREAN POWs

Father Emil Kapaun, an Army chaplain who died in a North Korean prisoner of war camp, is being promoted as a candidate for sainthood by one of his seminary classmates. Because of Fr Kapaun's countless acts of courage and compassion while a POW, others are alive today to tell the priest's inspiring story.

Msgr. Patrick J. Molloy, a St. Louis archdiocesan priest, is working with both the U.S. Archdiocese for the Military Services and Fr Kapaun's native Diocese of Wichita, Kan., to advance the cause of Fr Kapaun's canonisation. Publicizing his case, he also is searching for those willing to pray for a miracle through the chaplain's intercession.

Msgr. Molloy first heard about his classmate's extraordinary exploits when attending the 1957 dedication in Wichita of a high school named in Fr Kapaun's memory. At the event were several men who had been imprisoned with the priest.

"They all were in great admiration of what he had done," Msgr. Molloy recalled. He recently revisited the subject when reading a military newsletter given to him with a firsthand account of Fr Kapaun's life in the POW camp.

Fr Kapaun often represented the difference between life and death for many prisoners. He would organize raids on the enemy commissary, sometimes going alone, to help combat the devastating effects of dysentery on the men. The chaplain would bring back whatever food he could get to the starving Americans.

If caught, they would have been shot, "but they were never caught," Msgr. Molloy said. At the chaplain's direction, the POWs would pray to St. Dismas for protection. The saint, known as "the good thief," was one of two men crucified with Christ who asked his forgiveness and was promised paradise.

Due to dysentery, the POWs often lost control of their bodily functions. When they were too weak to take care of themselves, it was Fr Kapaun, whom the men called "padre," who carried them to the latrine and cleaned their soiled clothes. These and other acts of love endeared him to the men, the priest said.

While imprisoned, the POWs often grew depressed. "When the men lost hope, they would just sit down and look at the wall," Msgr. Molloy said. "They were just impervious to anything that was said or done, and they died. They gave up."

A Protestant chaplain, with a family back home, began staring at the wall. The men tried everything they could to persuade him to live. Then they called in Fr Kapaun. He knew that "the deepest thing in a man who is really religious (would be) his faith," Msgr. Molloy said. "So he said simply, 'I always said those Protestants were no damn good.' Right away, he reacted. The adrenaline began to work."

The Protestant chaplain survived, was freed at war's end and returned home. "And he gives Emil credit for saving his life. Some of the fellas," Msgr. Molloy added with a laugh, "when they told the story, said, 'This might stop him from being canonized.'"

After several months in camp, Fr Kapaun became ill from phlebitis, which proved fatal. Eventually he was taken away to die. "As he was being carried out by the guards, they said he asked their pardon for anything that he may have done that offended them," Msgr. Molloy said. The chaplain died on the 6th May, 1951, at age 35.

The North Koreans were glad to see Fr Kapaun die because he had kept up the men's spirits. The guards thought now they could break the other men. But they failed to take into account the priest's ability to bolster the men's morale even after his death.

Through Fr Kapaun's example, the men learned to take care of one another rather than resort to the then-common practice of every man for himself. The number of survivors at Fr Kapaun's POW camp was seven times greater than at other North Korean prison camps.

After Fr Kapaun's death, a young Jewish Marine was placed in the POW camp. He couldn't understand why the men were taking care of each other, unlike other places he had been held captive. When he asked why, everyone responded, "Padre Kapaun, Padre Kapaun."

The Marine was so moved by the chaplain's inspiration that he made a crucifix in the priest's memory out of native wood, using barbed wire as a crown of thorns. The cross, which was dismantled and taken out in pieces by the POWs when they were freed, now resides at the high school bearing Fr Kapaun's name.

For additional information, contact: Father John Hotze: e-mail hotze@cdowk.org or website: http://www.frkapaun.org

PRAYER

Lord Jesus, in the midst of the folly of war, your servant, Chaplain Emil Kapaun spent himself in total service to you on the battlefields and in the prison camps of Korea, until his death at the hands of his captors.

We now ask you, Lord Jesus, if it be your will, to make known to all the world the holiness of Chaplain Kapaun and the glory of his complete sacrifice for you by signs of miracles and peace.

In your name, Lord, we ask, for you are the source of peace, the strength of our service to others, and our final hope.

Amen. Chaplain Kapaun, pray for us.

H.M. The Queen and the Duke of Edinburgh paid an official call to the Vatican and met with **Pope John XXIII** on the 5th May 1961. The couple are seen here with the Pope on the last day of their three day state visit.

Fr D. McGuinness answers a query on dress, from the handbook from the Hostesses of the Guild of Our Lady of Ships, in September 1962.

The Knights of St. Columba perform a guard of honour as they kneel for **Cardinal Hinsley**, who in turn blesses them as he leaves the church of Our Lady of Good Counsel, Stoke Newington, north London, after the opening Mass in December 1938.

"The newly-appointed U.S. Ambassador to London is a Catholic," *The Universe* proudly announced in January 1938. **Mr. Joseph P. Kennedy** was Chairman of the U.S. Maritime Commission at the time, and is pictured here with his wife and nine children. Mr. Kennedy is seated *(left)*, on the arm of his chair is Patricia (13); behind Patricia is John F. (20); seated at her father's feet is Jean (9); and behind Jean is Eunice (16). With Mrs Kennedy *(extreme right)* are: Joseph Jnr. (22); Rosemary (19) standing next to her brother; Robert (12) leaning against fireplace; seated beside Robert is Kathleen (17) while Edward (6) is seated in front of his mother.

Lawyers in prayer at their annual Red Mass in Westminster Cathedral in October 1938. The Mass requests guidance from the Holy Spirit for all who seek justice, and offers the opportunity to reflect on what Catholics believe is the God-given power and responsibility of all in the legal profession. The Red Mass is so-called from the red vestments traditionally worn as a symbol of the tongues of fire that descended on the Apostles.

ARCHBISHOP AT WAR

The *Universe* photographer caught this charming and unusual study of Archbishop (later Cardinal) Bernard Griffin in January 1944. As Auxiliary Archbishop of Birmingham at the time he was making his contribution to the local war effort as an air raid warden.

Bernard William, Cardinal Griffin (21st February 1899 – 19th August 1956) was born in Birmingham, where his father was a carpenter turned city councillor and justice of the peace. The young Bernard won a scholarship to the local grammar school but his desire to be a priest led him to transfer to Cotton College in Staffordshire.

When the First World War broke out he joined the Royal Navy Air Service, but during this time he suffered a heart attack, which he concealed from doctors in order to avoid a discharge which he feared would prevent his acceptance for the priesthood. After the war he went to Oscott College, and was ordained priest on the 1st November 1924.

He then worked as private secretary to Archbishop John McIntyre of Birmingham until 1937. From 1929 to 1938, he served as diocesan chancellor of Birmingham, director of studies of the Catholic Evidence Guild, and Catholic representative on the BBC's religious advisory committe.

On the 26th May 1938 he was appointed Auxiliary Bishop of Birmingham and Titular Bishop of Appia. Pope Pius XII raised Griffin to Archbishop of Westminster on 18th December 1943. As Cardinal, he took a keen interest in the rebuilding of post-war Britain, arguing especially for the provision of Catholic schools, and was seen by some as liberal in areas of social principles. He died from a heart attack in 1956, aged 57.

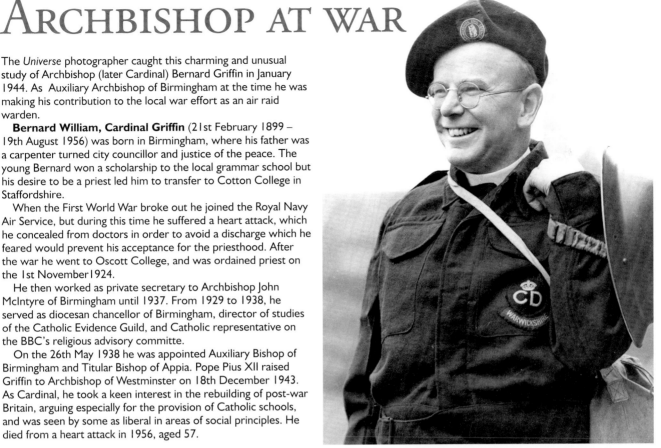

There was no shortage of volunteers when St. Anthony's RC Church, Preston, decided to celebrate a monthly 'folk' Mass. The group of musicians, known as 'St. Anthony's Folk' was started in 1972 by Fr. Peter Sayer, and was run by husband and wife team Tom and Kath Smyth. As well as performing at Mass the group were also in demand for concerts, weddings, funerals and even a Lourdes rally. They are pictured here in January 1967, having just finished work on a 14-track LP of songs and hymns.

Patrick Flynn, a grave digger in Kensal Green cemetery, London, started his work every morning with a prayer at the grave of Margaret Sinclair, the humble Poor Clare who died in 1925. This picture was taken in December 1927, just after he'd helped exhume her body for return to Edinburgh.

Playing pied pipers at St. John Fisher school, Preston, in October 1972, were pipers Ian Rogers *(left)* of Glasgow, and David Salkeld, of Musselburgh. They piped pupils into the school wh sich had been selected as the first call for men of the Scots Guards on a goodwill tour of the North West. As well as static displays, the pupils were treated to an hour-long concert by the band of the Scots Guards and a marching display.

Archbishop McDonald of St. Andrews and Edinburgh *(right)*, and Bishop Myers, Auxiliary to the Cardinal Archbishop of Westminster, watching a pageant play performed by the Grail girls at Schiedam, Holland during Catholic celebrations in May 1933.

141

THOUSANDS ARE SAILING ...

The faded green card pictured here is one of the most cherished posessions of Joseph Kelly, CEO and editor of *The Universe* Catholic weekly.

Joseph's maternal grandparents were born at the very end of the 19th century, into poor Catholic farming families in Ballinabarney, on the slopes of the famous Wicklow Gap in Ireland.

James Walsh moved first to London, where he courted and married his childhood sweetheart, Kathleen Hickey.

Life in 1930s London was almost as hard as it had been in rural Ireland, and Jim – like so many Irishmen of his generation – dreamed of the fabled golden pavements across the Atlantic.

On the 12th March, 1929, Jim presented himself to the American Embassy in London, and came away with his cherished 'green card'. Five months later he was disembarking at Ellis Island, having left behind, in a strange city, a young wife and two year old daughter, Eileen.

On old friend, Partick J. Hempenstall, had already gone to America, and was doing very well for himself in New York. Patrick had offered Jim lodgings at his home at 2831 Boadway, but Jim could not afford the passage for both himself and his family.

"It's hard for us to imagine the dreadful circumstances that drove so many young families like my grandad's to part, in the hope that the husband might carve out a new life for his dependants," said Joseph.

"Sadly, the immigrations records I searched through looking for my grandparents revealed that many, many steerage passengers from Ireland were husbands with families back home, or women and children travelling alone," said Joseph.

Jim worked at various day jobs in New York, and at night gained qualifications from the city's Murray Hill Evening Trade School. Eventually he found a permanent position as an apprenticed electrical engineer at the Hays Building, in Maiden Lane.

Twelve months later he was finally able to send enough money back home to enable his wife and young daughter to set sail for the promised land, as third class passangers aboard the Cunard liner, *Aquitania*.

A postcard sent to her best friend by jim's wife, just a few days after she arrived, still survives. It gives a vivid snapshot of how tough the six week journey was for this young mother and her two year old:

"115 - 17 East 96 Street, New York City. Sunday. Dearest Ethel, Just a few lines to say I arrived here safely. I had a nasty voyage got bitten all over the first night on steamer with bugs. Had to stay in bed my body was poisoned was sick every day and not too well yet will write you a long letter later as I do not know your address. Will post this to Reigate. Write me a line soon dearest Ethel. Hoping you and Wilfred had a nice holiday. Much love from your dear friend Kathleen, xxxx, and from Eileen."

Jim Walsh's 'green card' was vaild for five years, and during that time he completed an apprenticeship, and became a valued member of the maintainance staff at the Hays. He seems to have warmed to New York life, as the family moved several times, each time to a bigger and better apartment in the city.

"I can remember my grandad telling me fantastical stories about their time in America," said Joseph.

"He marvelled at 'the Silver Bullet train' standing in Grand Central Station, and he never forgot an excursion to Niagra Falls. He bought a glass paperweight at the Falls, which I still have on my desk to this day".

Kathleen found life more difficult, and yearned for her relations back in Ireland.

In 1935 Jim's visa finally expired, and he made one desperate attempt to get it extended for another year so that he could at least finish his apprenticeship.

In early 1936 Kate became pregnant again, leaving them with a dilemma – their child would have US and not Irish citizenship, making a return to Ireland difficult.

For an heartbreaking second time, Jim and Kate were parted, and she returned to friends in London, again crossing the Atlantic alone, this time six months pregnant, and clutching an eight year old child.

James Walsh finished his apprenticeship, and left New York with a heavy heart in June 1935. An open reference from the superintendent at the Hays Building, a Mr. S. Heppel, states: *"It gives me great pleasure to be able to write a tribute to such a deserving person. He left my employ because he wished to join his wife in Europe, which only proves the sterling quality of his character."*

Jim and Kate settled eventually and saw out their days in Somerset, England, where they both sleep untroubled today, side by side, their long journey over.

Their two daughters live outside London.

"It's funny to think that, but for a few twists of fate, I might have been a New

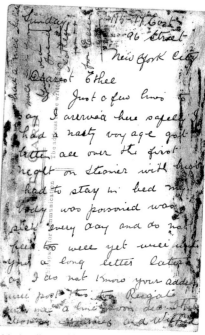

Yorker," says *Universe* editor Joseph Kelly.

More on this story at:
www.corglancy.net

A British cruiser rescued these French children from Boulogne when France fell in June 1940. They were pictured shortly before being taken to safety "somewhere in Scotland" under the care of French Sisters of Charity.

A day out on the river for the Poor Servants of the Mother of God from hospitals in Liverpool and St. Helens in 1973.

The charred crucifix of the Church of Our Lady of Victories, Kensington, London, after German bombers struck on the night of the 13th September 1940. During a large-scale air raid, the church was struck by two oil bombs, which gutted the 70 year old church, and also destroyed the Carmelite church on nearby Kensington Church Street.

Later in the war Derek Worlock, Archbishop of Liverpool, was appointed a curate of the church under Canon Walton and he recalled in his sermon at the 25th anniversary of the church in 1984: "We became firm friends from the moment when, a few days after my arrival, I had to fling him (Canon Walton) to the floor as he hung out of the landing window to try to see the flying bomb which seconds later crashed into the road between Lyons and Troy Court.

"I fell on top of the Canon as the glass came in to cover both of us .... We worked together most of that afternoon trying to get people, alive and dead, out of the wreckage around what is now your church. It launched me on my record of giving the Last Sacraments over 50 times before I had a case of natural death ..."

Sunday Mass was celebrated initially at the Odeon Cinema only a few yards away from the ruins and later, following the closure of

the Odeon, at the Cavendish Furnishing Company on the High Street (now Safeways) who kindly provided a temporary home for the congregation at a rent of one shilling per year!

Services continued there until November of 1942 when services transferred both to the parish hall at the back of the bombed church and to the chapel at the Covent of the Assumption in Kensington Square.

It was to this makeshift accommodation that Monsignor Canon John Bagshawe was greeted when he was appointed parish priest in October 1952. He was charged by Cardinal Griffin with the task of rebuilding Our Lady of Victories.

In the same year, Adrian Gilbert Scott was instructed to design the new church on the old site. He took his inspiration from the previous church in designing a long-aisled nave with a short chancel and flanking chapels.

A distinct feature of his design was the large crypt under the church, which was the first part of the building to come into service. The first design was more extravagant than he one actually built.

The final design was built in common brick during 1955-1958 with only the entrance elevation being finished in facing bricks.

A remarkably poignant study of the Bishop of Northampton, **Dr. Cary-Elwes,** lying on a stretcher on the platform at Victoria station in September 1931. His Lordship had been leading a pilgrimage to Lourdes, but suffered a heart attack on the outward journey and received Extreme Unction on the train. Dr. Cary-Elwes made a brief recovery, but died in May the follwing year.

Manchester prepared a rousing welcome for **Cardinal Bourne** on his arrival at the city's Central station in October 1926. A Scout guard of honour was drawn up on the platform, and cheering crowds waited outside the barriers.

(*Main picture*) Sir William pictured during his 1933 tour of the depressed industrial areas of the UK. (*Inset*) As Conservative MP for Brighton, Pavilion. (*Above*) Teeling as drawn by the newspaper's travelling artist on the 1933 Universe Unemployed Men's Pilgrimage to Rome.

ALLY OF THE IRISH IMMIGRANT

Sir **Luke William Burke Teeling** (5th February 1903 – 26th October 1975) was an Irish author, traveller and United Kingdom politician. He was known for his enthusiasm for a Channel Tunnel.

He was born in Dublin to a prominent Catholic family, and was the son of the Accountant-General of the Irish Supreme Court. Family legend has it that one of his great-granduncles, Bartholomew Teeling, was hanged by the British for taking part in the Irish Rebellion of 1798. He attended the London Oratory School and Magdalen College, Oxford where he studied history.

On leaving university, Teeling became a journalist and travelled widely both at home and abroad, especially in the United States where he described himself as an "amateur tramp". He lived among the homeless and hitched lifts on freight trains, reporting back to *The Times* and *The Universe* about his adventures.

In the early 1930s he also studied the youth movements in Nazi Germany. In January 1933, disguised as a tramp, he toured the depressed industrial areas of the UK. sleeping in casual wards and doss-houses, trying to get work. He told *The Universe* that, in six weeks' travelling, the only two offers he received were as a ventriloquist's assistant and a "quack oculist's partner".

He also took part in the 1933 *Universe* Unemployed Men's Pilgrimage to Rome, and was chairman of the executive committee of the Catholic Emigration Society.

In winter 1933 he walked all the way from London to Newcastle-upon-Tyne, sleeping in hostels and examining the efforts of local councils to tackle unemployment.

Another preoccupation when Teeling was travelling abroad was the treatment given to Irish immigrants and to the Catholic Church.

In 1937 he wrote *The Pope in Politics*, which suggested that Pope Pius XI was opposed to the new forms of Catholicism developing in the Americas. He followed this in 1939 with *Crisis for Christianity*, on the relations between the Catholic Church and Nazism.

When the Second World War broke out, Teeling joined the Royal Air Force. Having already fought the safe Labour seat of West Ham Silvertown in the 1929 general election, he was elected to Parliament as a Conservative for Brighton in a 1944 by-election.

This was a two-member seat, and Teeling was re-elected in the 1945 general election. The seat was divided into two individual constituencies thereafter, and Teeling was chosen for Brighton Pavilion.

Throughout his Parliamentary career he remained on the backbenches, but his expertise on foreign affairs was acknowledged (he was a Freeman of Seoul in Korea). He was a strong supporter of all attempts to build a tunnel under the English Channel, and chaired an all-party committee which campaigned for it. He was also Secretary of the All-Party committee on holiday resorts, and was knighted in 1962.

The great Irish tenor, Count John McCormack, reflects for a moment before getting up to sing at an open air High Mass in Los Angeles, in October 1937, in front of a crowd of 20,000 Catholics.

Mrs. Mary McAleese, editing *Till Death Us Do Part*, a video guide to marriage produced by Veritas, the Dublin publishers. In the video Mrs. McAleese talked to young people whose marriages have broken down, and to a couple who considered separation.

Mary McAleese was born Mary Patricia Leneghan in Belfast. She was educated at Queen's University and Trinity College, Dublin. Called to the Northern Ireland Bar in 1974 she is also a member of the Bar in the Republic. In 1976 she married Martin McAleese and in 1979 joined RTÉ as a journalist and presenter. During this period she also wrote for *The Universe* Catholic newspaper.

She became President of the Irish Republic in 1997, taking over from Mrs. Mary Robinson, who had also been her predecessor as Reid Professor of Criminal Law, Criminology and Penology at Trinity 20 years previously.

Mrs. McAleese was elected unopposed for a second term of office in 2004. She is the first person born in Ulster to become President of the Republic. She is currently the longest serving elected female Head of State anywhere in the world.

(Above) Rome City Commissioner Francesco Diana presents **Rt. Rev. Mgr. John Patrick Carroll-Abbing**, a native of Ireland, with a specially cast gold medal to commemorate the 25th anniversary of his ordination to the priesthood in 1960. Following the liberation of Rome in 1944 Mgr. Carroll-Abbing founded the first of his Boys' Town's, or 'Shoeshine Hotels' as they were popularly known, to cater for the disposessed population of street children in the city left orphaned and homeless by the war. At the time of his death in 2001 the Boys' Town's and Girls' Town organisations where the oldest American charities working abroad.
(Below) Some of the first intake of 'ragazzi' welcomed off the streets of Rome in 1945.

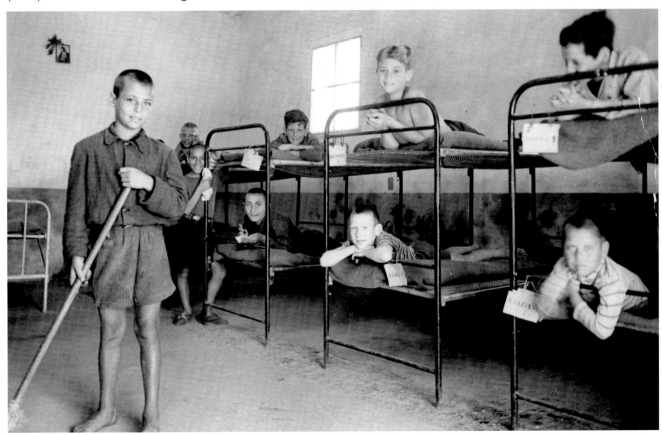

"Polish boys from Siberian ice-fields and Turkestan marshes – boys who before they had reached their teens were left alone in the world and saved their lives only by using their own wits in the midst of war-created chaos – are among this smart, happy-looking section of a junior apprentice wing of the RAF in Great Britain. They reached safety here, 204 of them, after travelling thousands of miles in the worst conditions in the wake of the Polish army. With home gone, parents dead and all traces of birth certificates vanished, many of them do not even know their own ages. In Britain they are learning to be good Poles, efficient airmen and mechanics and, with regular religious instructon, good Catholics." From *The Universe*, the 22nd October 1943.

The Children's Procession passing The Houses of Parliament during the Emancipation Congress, held in London in September 1929.

The scene outside Westminster Cathedral in May 1930, as Father (later Saint) **John Southworth**'s body was taken there for reburial. Southworth was a member of the Southworth family of Samlesbury Hall, Blackburn, he was ordained priest at the English College, Douai, and was sent on the mission, on the 13th October, 1619. He was arrested and condemned to death in Lancashire in 1627, and imprisoned first in Lancaster Castle, and afterwards in the Clink, London. In 1636 he had been released and was living at Clerkenwell, but frequently visited the plague-stricken dwellings of Westminster to convert the dying. He was arrested several times and, after his final apprehension, he was tried at the Old Bailey, and as he insisted on pleading "guilty" to being a priest. He was condemned, and died on the gallows at Tyburn, on the 28th June 1854. His remains passed to the Duke of Norfolk's family, who had them sent to the English College at Douai. They were hidden during the French Revolution, and were thought to have been lost, but they were dramatically rediscovered in 1927, and brought back to England, to be enshrined in Westminster. In 1970, John Southworth was canonised by Pope Paul VI among the Forty Martyrs of England and Wales, whose joint feast day is kept on the 25th October.

Some of the faithful are pictured outside London's Westminster Cathedral on the 27th January 1963, where they were waiting to file past the body of William Cardinal Godfrey, Archbishop of Westminster, who had died the previous week.

Fr. Bernard Egan S.J; who was the first paratroop chaplain to jump from a plane is seen here leaving Buckingham Palace in March 1944 after receiving the Military Cross from King George VI, for gallantry in Sicily.

Archbishop Andrew Joseph McDonald of St. Andrews and Edinburgh, with Monsignor McHardy and Canon Birnie, join a procession through Dunfermline in June 1937.

L ord and Lady Lovat, his son and and heir the Master of
Lovat and Miss Marjorie Eyston *(left)* pictured at the New
College and Magdalen College point-to-point at Little Tew,
Oxon in February 1933.

Just minutes after this picture was taken, Lord Lovat collapsed
and died. Simon Joseph Fraser, 14th Lord Lovat, DSO (1871-1933)
was a leading Roman Catholic aristocrat, landowner, and the 23rd
Chief of Clan Fraser. He was the son of Simon Fraser, 13th Lord
Lovat. While legally the 14th Lord, he was referred to as the 16th
Lord Lovat. He served in the 1st Life Guards. In 1899 he raised the
Lovat Scouts, who fought in the South African War.

In World War I, he commanded the Highland Mounted Brigade
and was awarded the D.S.O. He was succeeded by his eldest son
Simon as the 15th Lord Lovat (known as the 17th Lord) in 1933
who distinguished himself during the D-Day landings at Normandy
in June 1944 and his younger son Sir Hugh Fraser was a successful
politician.

Lord Lovat is a title in the Peerage of Scotland dating to 1458. It
is held along with the title of Baron Lovat in the Peerage of the
United Kingdom. In 1697, after the 9th Lord Lovat died, Simon
Fraser, his brother, kidnapped and forcefully married the late Lord's
widow, the former Lady Amelia Murray, only daughter of the 1st
Marquess of Atholl.

However, Lady Lovat's powerful family, the Murrays, were
angered, and prosecuted Fraser, who fled the country. Fraser was
convicted in absentia, attainted, and sentenced to death.

Due to his attainder, he could not succeed to the Lordship when
the 10th Lord, also his brother, died. In 1715, however, Fraser
supported the Government against a Jacobite uprising and was
rewarded by being pardoned for his crimes. In 1730, he won
litigation seeking to confirm his title of Lord Lovat. In 1745,
however, Lord Lovat participated in The '45 against the Crown and
was therefore sentenced to death. He was beheaded on Tower Hill
in London, becoming the last man to die in this manner.

His titles, furthermore, were forfeit. (He had been created Duke
of Fraser, Marquess of Beaufort, Earl of Stratherrick and Upper
Tarf, Viscount of the Aird and Strathglass and Lord Lovat and
Beaulieu in the Jacobite Peerage of Scotland by James Francis
Edward Stuart (titular King James III of England and VIII of Scotland)
in 1740.) Later, in 1837, Thomas Fraser, who would have
succeeded to the title but for the forfeiture, was created Baron
Lovat, of Lovat in the County of Inverness, in the Peerage of the
United Kingdom. In 1854, the attainder of the 11th Lord was
reversed, and Lord Lovat became the 12th Lord Lovat in the
Peerage of Scotland. The two peerages remain merged.

The numbering of the Scottish Lordship used by Clan Fraser
differs from the legal numbering in that it ignores the attainder of
1747-1854, with the result that the 16th Lord is termed by them
"18th Lord Lovat". The Lordship of Lovat has for some time been
linked to the Chiefship of Clan Fraser.

Nuns sit on a grassy slope during an ecumenical service at Avenham Park, near Preston, in September 1972.

The Irish Ambassador to London, **Mr J.G. Molloy**, hands over the Republican flag that had flown over the GPO on Easter Monday, 1916 to the Taoiseach Mr Seán Lemass, in March 1966, watched by Frank Aiken, Minister for External Affairs, and Flag Bearer Commandant Frank Neil.

The green battle-scarred flag was hauled down when the insurgents were forced to surrender the GPO to the 3rd Battalion, Royal Irish Regiment. It was later given to the Imperial War Museum in London. The Taoiseach had been writing to British Prime Minister Harold Wilson about the possible return of the iconic flag to Ireland.

Speaking at the handover, the Taoiseach said: "I want to express appreciation of the manner, the speed and generosity in which the British Government responded to my request that this flag should be restored to us in this year when we celebrate the 50th anniversary of the 1916 Rising."

THE MALINES CONVERSATIONS

F ew Catholics today will have heard of the the Malines Conversations, a series of informal discussions exploring possibilities of corporate reunion between the Catholic Church and the Church of England held in the Belgian primatial see of Malines (now normally referred to as Mechelen) from 1921 to 1927.

This early, ground-breaking attempt at high-level ecumenical dialogue was largely the initiative of of Désiré-Félicien-François-Joseph Cardinal Mercier, a brilliant but controversial Beligian prelate.

With tacit support from the Vatican and the Archbishops of Canterbury and York, Cardinal Mercier assembled on the Anglican side the future Lord Halifax, Bishops Frere and Gore, Armitage Robinson (Dean of Wells) and Dr. Kidd.

The Catholic participants included Mercier himself, Batiffol, Hemmer, Portal and Mercier's successor Van Roey, who was personally less favourable to the idea of unity than his predecessor.

Eventually, Cardinal Bourne of Westminster successfully urged the Vatican to withdraw its encouragement, in line with Leo XIII's Bull *Apostolicae Curae* (1896), which had denied validity to Anglican orders, and Van Roey wound up the conversations in 1927.

The dialogue is particularly remembered for Dom Lambert Beauduin's 1925 paper *L'église Anglicane unie, mais non absorbée* (The Anglican Church united, but not absorbed.)

Désiré Félicien François Joseph, Cardinal Mercier (21st November 1851–23rd January 1926) served as Archbishop of Mechelen from 1906 until his death, and was elevated to the cardinalate in 1907.

His comprehensive knowledge of St. Thomas Aquinas earned him the newly-erected chair of Thomism at the Louvain in 1882. It was in this post, which he retained until 1905, that he forged a lifelong friendship with Dom Columba Marmion, an Irish Thomist.

He founded in 1894 and edited until 1906 the *Revue Néoscholastique,* and wrote in a scholastic manner on metaphysics, philosophy, and psychology.

His reputation within his field obtained the recognition of Pope Pius X, and Mercier was appointed Archbishop of Mechelen and thus Primate of Belgium on the 7th February 1906. He was created Cardinal Priest of S. Pietro in Vincoli by Pope St. Pius X in the consistory of the 15th April 1907.

Mercier suffered from persistent dyspepsia, and in early January 1926 he underwent surgery for a lesion of the stomach. During surgery, the anaesthetised Cardinal even held a conversation with his surgeon. In his final days, he was visited by King Albert and Queen Elizabeth, Lord Halifax, and family members.

He entered a deep coma around 2pm on the 23rd January 1926, and died an hour later, aged 74. He is buried at St. Rumbold's Cathedral. Mechelen.

(Top) **The cardinal was a staunch supporter of the Catholic press, and sent this personally-written Chistmas card to The Universe in December 1919.**
(above) **Members of the British War Cabinet pose for a group shot before a meeting in London, on the 8th November 1939. Lord Halifax is seated, 1st left.**

The Australian cricket captain, Ian William Geddes Johnson, shakes hands with his host, the **Duke of Norfolk**, before a match between the visiting Australians and the Duke of Norfolk's XI at Arundel Park, Sussex in May 1956. It was the Australians' first match of a UK tour.

The Duke of Norfolk's XI is a scratch cricket team, originally named for the 16th Duke but, following his death in 1975, the team played on in his widow's name as Lavinia, Duchess of Norfolk's XI. After her own death in 1995, the title reverted to the original, in the name of the 17th (until 2002) and then 18th

Dukes. The English international summer has traditionally been marked by a fixture between this team and the tourists at Arundel Castle, the seat of the Catholic Dukes of Norfolk.

Indeed the team has played almost all its matches in England at that ground, although one match against the International Cavaliers in 1966 was played at Hove.

The team was typically largely made up of county players not involved in other games, mixed with recently retired internationals. Derek Randall, Robin Smith and Andy Flower are among those to have played for the Duke's team.

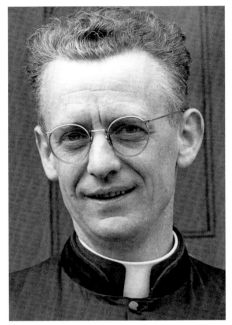

The Rev. Dr. (later Cardinal) **John C.Heenan**, pictured in 1947, the day before leaving his duties as parish priest at St. Nicholas, Manor Park, London E12, for an extensive lecture tour of America, after which he returned to become Superior of the Catholic Missionary Society of Great Britain.

As a tribute to Archbishop Whiteside, whose body had been entombed in the crypt of Lutyens' grand Liverpool cathedral project, workmen engaged in building work in January 1937 placed flowers on his tomb every week. The crypt - which lies underneath the present structure – was the only element completed before costs became prohibitive.

Pilgrims arrive at Walsingham in April 1948, having walked barefoot along the Holy Mile from the Friday market to the Slipper Chapel.

Eleven brothers and sisters – including three priests and five nuns – met for the first time in many years for the funeral of their mother, Mrs. Helena Bluett, of Kilmallock, Co. Limerick, in January 1970. *(Pictured from left)*: Fr. James Bluett, parish priest of Kilmeedy, Co. Limerick; Sr. Mary Clare, Sisters of Charity, Charleville, Co. Cork; Mr. Thomas Bluett, retired farmer, Kilmallock; Canon Patrick Bluett, parish priest of St. Mary's, Market Weighton, Yorks; Sr. Hilda, Irish Sisters of Charity, Dublin; Sr. Francis Therese, Buttevant, Co. Cork, Sr. Frances Bernadette, Chester; Fr. John Bluett, parish priest Good Shepherd, Downham, Kent; Sr. Magdalen Regis, St. Vincent's, Cork; Miss Joan Bluett, assistant matron, Barrington's Hospital, Limerick, and Mr. William Bluett, businessman, of Charville, Co. Cork.

The Queen and the Duke of Edinburgh, followed by their entourage, leave St. Peter's Basilica, escorted by Swiss Guards, after their first visit to Pope John XXIII. The Queen wore a black lace gown and veil topped by a diamond tiara for her 20 minute historic meeting with the pontiff. The British royal couple were on a state visit to Italy.

Sadly this photograph is undated, but it shows **Bishop Derek Worlock** arriving at Newman College, Birmingham.
(Note the very appropriate car registration number: NOE I.) Derek Worlock was ordained to the priesthood in 1944 in Westminster
Cathedral, and shortly afterwards was appointed private secretary to Cardinal Griffin. He assisted successive cardinals for some 19 years.
He attended every session of the Second Vatican Council between 1962 and 1965, the year in which he was appointed Bishop of
Portsmouth. In 1976 he was appointed Archbishop of Liverpool. In January 1994 he was awarded the Freedom of the City of Liverpool.
He was made Companion of Honour in the 1996 New Year's Honours List, but died of lung cancer four days after his 76th birthday,
just a week before he was due to receive the honour.

Father Filmer, Master of the Guild of our Lady of Ransom, with altar servers bearing martyr's palms, leads the Tyburn Walk in May 1933.

Amazing what you find in the waste bin – this image had been discarded in our archives because someone had attempted to retouch Chesterton's suit, and ended up spilling bleach over the print! Thankfully, modern technology has enabled us to retouch and re-build the damaged suit.

It's February 1927, and the Bishop of Northampton has arrived to open St. Theresa's Church, Beaconsfield, where previously parishioners had to celebrate Mass in The Railway Hotel.

According to the *Universe* reporter who attended: "The church is unfurnished, and will be nearly double the present length when completed." **Mr. G.K. Chesterton**, who lived nearby was present at the opening. This picture shows *(from left)* "GKC"; Mr. S.G. Butler FRIBA, the architect; Dudley Charles Cary-Elwes, Bishop of Northampton; Fr. T. Walker, Rector of High Wycombe; and Fr. W.S. Bainbridge, who had been assigned to serve the new church from High Wycombe.

Three year old **John Earle** visits the replica grotto of Lourdes, which had been erected on a piece of derelict land belonging to St. Joesph's Church in Redhill, Surrey, in March 1963. According to the parish priest, Fr. Daniel O'Kane, the grotto was a full sized replica of the one at Lourdes, and the money to build it "has been raised by a church-run football pool."

Women praying for **Pope Pius XI** in Westminster cathedral during his final hours in February 1939. The 81 year old pontiff had refused to take to his bed till three days before his death, stricken by cardiac asthma and kidney disturbances.

A sturdy patient, he had told his physician that "the Pope must not stay in bed. The Pope must be Pope."

Mindful of Leo XIII, who lay 20 days a-dying, he had said: "I will die sulla breccia" – in the breach.

On the morning of the 14th February, in an agony of effort, while the others wept, the Pope summoned his strength to make this last, supreme gesture. He lifted his right hand, mumbled a blessing. Falteringly his hand signalled its last apostolic benediction, and fell back on the bed.

He mumbled something. To some it seemed he said: "Jesus and Mary. . . . Peace to the world."

Others thought they heard him say: "In our last rites . . . Sister Therese of the Infant Jesus . . . art near to us. God is merciful. May His will be done."

But all were agreed that earlier, the Pope's last articulate words had been: "I still have so many things to do."

A fabulous study of the great Catholic writer, and *Universe* columnist, **Hilaire Belloc**. Sadly, the image is undated.

(Above) Whilst visiting a war cemetery in Normandy in February 1993, **Fr Kevin Vesey**, an army chaplain, came across the grave of Fr. Gerard Nesbitt, a priest killed in action in 1944 during the liberation of France.

Fr. Vesey was astonished to find that Fr. Nesbitt had served at St. Patrick's, Felling, on Tyneside, the first parish in which he himself had served. Fr. Nesbitt was 33, the son of Stephen and Joan Nesbitt, and had been awarded the Croix de Guerre.

"In a different time, and a different place, we could have exchanged roles. I was struck by the sacrifice of people my own age in a different generation," Fr. Vesey told *The Universe*.

Fr. Vesey was accompanying solidiers of 73 Field Squardon, Royal Engineers, who were retracing the unit's steps from D-Day to its disbanding at Rendsburg, Germany, in 1945.

The Right Reverend Thomas Dunn (Right) was the fifth Bishop of Nottingham, serving from 25th Feb 1916 to his death on the 21st September 1931.

Thomas Dunn was born on 25th July 1870 in London and educated in Beaumont College, Hammersmith, and in Rome at the Academia. He was ordained priest on the 2nd February 1892 and appointed secretary to Cardinal Vaughan 1893-1903. In 1902 he was appointed a canon, and in 1906 he was put in charge of the Mission at Staines.

Canon Dunn was appointed fifth Bishop of Nottingham in 1915 and was ordained by Cardinal Bourne at Westminster on the 25th February 1916.

Bishop Dunn found a rapidly growing diocese and encouraged church building on an unprecedented scale. The work of religious orders was given fresh impetus – the arrival of the Assumptionists to the Becket School was in 1931 – and new parishes were established all over the diocese.

Bishop Dunn paid particular attention to his cathedral, seeking to restore all things in Pugin style, and made efforts to restore Gregorian Chant to the cathedral's Liturgy. During Bishop Dunn's time in Nottingham there was an increase in vocations and 34 priests were ordained for the diocese.

Early in autumn 1931, Bishop Dunn's health began to deteriorate and he died on the 21st September 1931; he was buried in the cathedral crypt.

The boys of St. Richard's School, Bexhill, Sussex, had plenty to hum about in June 1978 when they built the Bee *(left)*, a city car that won them a prize for the best use of space in the BP School Buildacar 1976 contest. Inspired by this success the boys bult the Mindion *(right)*, "a stylish modern car" for the 1978 contest. The cars were pictured here at the Sussex University exhibition, with Mr. Peter Fairhurst, the teacher responsible for their conception. The two boys are Neil Crossinggum, 15 *(left)* and Perry Jordan, 14.

It was gruelling work for this group of Benedictine monks who were making a road to the site of a new abbey they were building for themselves at Buckfast in Devon in May 1939.

Bomb damage to the high altar at the French Church in London's Leicester Square in November 1940.

SECRET
MISSION
FRIENDS SMUGGLED ROBE TO ARCHBISHOP

In 1947, when brother Ivankovich fled Yugoslavia, the country was under communist iron rule. The Catholic Church was considered the major enemy of the regime. Its clergy were systematically persecuted and decimated.

The Partisans once entered the Franciscan Monastery in Siroki Brijeg, doused 14 friars with petrol and set them afire. In 1951, of the 151 priests the Senj Diocese who were there before the war, only 88 survived. But the biggest thorn for the Communists was Archbishop Alojzije Stepinac. When in a pastoral letter he stated that since the Communist take-over, 273 clergy had been killed, 169 more were imprisoned and 89 were missing, it was the excuse the regime was looking for. They tried the Archbishop and sentenced him to 16 years in prison.

Brother Ivan Ivankovich was from Medjugorie, now known throughout the world for Blessed Mother's apparitions. When Medjugorje's pastor was killed, he decided to flee. His half-brother was killed, his mother spent three months in jail. His father was severely beaten on the kitchen floor and denied medical aid.

After two years in hiding, brother Ivankovich escaped to Rome, where he met Father Ivan Tomas of the Croatian Radio Program of the Vatican who found Ivan a job at the Croatian College of St. Jerome in Rome.

Ivankovich spent two years at St. Jerome and received religious guidance from Fr Tomas. After that, he emigrated to America and met a wonderful couple in the San Francisco area, Aaron and Frances Chilcoat, who opened their hearts and their home to a refugee and witnessed his swearing in as a new American citizen.

When **Frances Chilcoat**, a Slovenian, retired from her job of nine years at United Airlines in 1954, the company presented her with a 30-day employee travel pass. She decided to visit her father's relatives in Yugoslavia.

The trip had mysterious trapping from the very beginning. When Frances went to the Yugoslavian Consulate in San Francisco to pick up her visa, she recalls a tall hulking official sternly warning her she had better not step out of line.

"He told me even though she was a U.S. citizen, I would become Yugoslavia's property once I arrived there. It was a pretty scary meeting."

When she later told her husband, Aaron, he asked her not to go. At this point, Frances was beginning to have second thoughts, too. But then **Grace Norton**, a friend from the airlines, offered to go along, if they could visit Rome.

Unknown to everyone, the two women had also agreed to smuggle a cardinal's robe into Yugosavia for the then Archbishop Stepinac.

Cardinal Stepinac was beatified on October 4, 1998. An estimated 400,000 people attended the ceremony in Zagreb, Croatia, which was conducted by Pope John Paul II.

Frances, who now resides in Burlingame, CA., said: "Ifelt so good when he was beatified. It pleased me to think he was able to be buried in his robe. The one I had smuggled from Italy."

(Above) Frances, on the right, is pictured with Grace Norton and Father Ivan Tomas at St. Peter's Basilica in 1954. The photo was taken just before the two American women agreed to smuggle a red cardinal's robe for Zagreb Archbishop Aloysius Stepinac into communist-controlled Yugoslavia.

(Left) Priests pray around the glass sarcophagus of Cardinal Alojzije Stepinac, in the cathedral of Zagreb on the 1st October, the day before the pope's arrival in Croatia. The cardinal is adorned in his 'smuggled' robe.

The great granddaughter of Chales Dickens, **Miss Monica Dickens**, a Catholic, posed for *The Universe* in May 1939, to mark the publication of her first book, *One Pair of Hands*. After leaving school she was presented at court as a debutante, but decided to go into service despite coming from the privileged class; her experiences as a cook and general servant formed the nucleus of her book.

On a bright summer's morning in 1970, the monks of Pluscarden Abbey, near Elgin, take to the fields to help gather in the harvest.

In February 1968 violent storms hit Scotland, and this was all that remained of the Catholic club at Port Glasgow, which had only been completed a month earlier by the Knights of St. Columba. Invitations for the opening had been sent to Bishop Black of Paisley, the Supreme Knight, the Provost of the town and other dignitaries.

(Left) This unusual November study reproduced in *The Universe* in 1938 was taken at St. Ninian's Cemetery, Banffshire, in the Catholic heartland of north east Scotland, of which the caption says: "in the past gave eight bishops and nearly 100 priests to the Church. Here are buried Bishop Nicholson, first Vicar Apostolic of Scotland, who died in 1719, also 26 other priests whose names are recorded on the cross in the centre of the picture. Close by is the chapel of Tynet, the oldest post-Reformation church in Scotland." The figure in the picture is **Peter Anson**, *The Universe* Pilgrim Artist.

(Right) **Brother John Ogilvie** of Pluscarden Abbey demonstrates the pure beeswax polish that the monks were manufacturing in 1990.

In December 1943 the newly-formed Catholic Committee for Relief Abroad held its first meeting at the offices of the Catholic Women's League in London. It was the official constituent body of the Council for British Societies for Relief Abroad formed in the Autumn of 1942 at the British government's suggestion to pool their experiences and co-ordinate their efforts "in the liberated countries". Sir Cecil Dormer, former Ambassador to Poland, was the committee's chairman, and the Vice chairman was the Hon. Mrs. Woodruff, (seated extreme left) national president to the CWL. Also in this photograph (but sadly not indicated) are Bishop Mathew, Canon George Craven, Mrs. Arnold Toynbee (general secretary), Mrs. Leigh White, Mrs. Skeet (hon. secretary), Miss Barbara Ward, Mrs. Given Wilson (chairman of the Westminster CWL), Mrs. Cowper, Lady Rendel, Lady Holberton and Mr. A.F. Loveday (hon. treasurer).

Two women received the title of Lady of the Holy Sepulchre of Jerusalem in Westminster Cathedral on the 4th November 1955. **Miss Holland** was well known for her work with Lourdes pilgrimages, and **Dr. Dorothy Makepeace** was Senior Inspector at the Children's Department of the Home office.

The great Irish tenor, **Count John McCormack**, reading his *Universe* before a performance in London in January 1928. The singer was a regular reader, and in December 1930 broke off from a world tour to sing for the staff of the newspaper at their 70 year celebratory dinner.

Recreation time for the Poor Clares of Woodchester convent, Stroud, in November 1982.

Mr. and Mrs. G.K. Chesterton pictured relaxing at home in December 1938.

A suberbly executed photo-portrait of the **Most Rev. Dr. Edward Mulhern**, Bishop of Dromore, (Bishop: 31st Jan 1916 to 1943) taken at the legendary Keogh Studios, St. Stephen's Green, Dublin, some time around 1917.

Amongst his many notable achievements, Bishop Mulhern intervened in the Irish peace negotiations in August 1921, coming to Dublin one night with a message "from the highest authority" which he delivered personally to Eamon de Valera and other Sinn Fein leaders.

There were long consultations over the message – a priest accompanying the bishop was asked if the message had come from Cardinal Logue, the Primate of Ireland, to which he had replied "in the negative", leading some to conclude that Rome had intervened directly in the peace negotiatons.

Seminarians go down a mine as part of their Young Christian Worker training in October 1950. During that year students from several Catholic seminaries toured shipyards and factories to obtain first-hand knowledge of the conditions and problems of the workers.

The Little Sisters of the Poor, who were extending St. Anne's home for old people in Stoke Newington, London, in May 1971, benefitted from a Catholic Stage Guild concert that included the great pianist Semprini and the popular singer Bruce Trent.

CATHOLIC VC

Captain David Jamieson joined the illustrious ranks of Catholics awarded the Victoria Cross, after bravely holding a bridgehead in Normandy for 36 hours. He is pictured here at Buckingham Palace with his parents after receiving his VC medal in November 1944.

Captain Jamieson won the Victoria Cross for the magnificent leadership and courage he displayed in the desperate battle for the bridgehead on the River Orne in Normandy, which had been gained in August 1944 by the men of The Royal Norfolk Regiment during the breakout after the D-Day landings.

The citation for his VC read: "Throughout the 36 hours of bitter and close fighting, and in spite of the pain of his wounds, Captain Jamieson showed superb qualities of leadership and great personal bravery.

There were times when the position appeared hopeless, but on each occasion it was restored by his coolness and determination. He personally was largely responsible for the holding of this important bridgehead over the River Orne and for the repulse of seven German counter-attacks with great loss to the enemy."

David Auldjo Jamieson, the son of Sir Archibald Jamieson, KBE, MC, was born in 1920 and educated at Eton. He would have gone up to Cambridge University had the war not intervened.

After the war he became an instructor at the School of Infantry, Warminster, as a major; and in 1948 he was posted as adviser on the British Military Mission to Egypt. He resigned his commission that year to go into business in the United Kingdom and Australia.

He was a director of the Australian Agricultural Co from 1949 to 1978, and governor from 1952 to 1976. He was also a director of the UK branch of the Australian Mutual Provident Society, 1963-8 (deputy chairman 1973-89); of National Westminster Bank, 1983-87; and of Steetly plc, 1976-86 (deputy chairman, 1983-86).

In 1969 he became one of Her Majesty's Body Guard of the Honourable Corps of Gentlemen at Arms. In 1979-80 he was High Sheriff of Norfolk. In 1986 he delivered up his Stick of Office as Clerk of the Cheque and Adjutant on his appointment as Lieutenant of the Corps of Gentlemen at Arms, serving in that office until 1990, when he was appointed CVO.

For many years Jamieson and his family lived at The Drove House, in the peaceful west Norfolk village of Thornham, before settling at Burnham Market, in north Norfolk.

In his later years he bore with fortitude and cheerfulness the successive amputation of both legs.

His first wife, Nancy Elwes, whom he married in Sydney in 1948, was killed in a road accident in 1963. They had a son and two daughters. He married in 1969 Joanna, a daughter of Edward Woodall.

David Jamieson died on the 5th May 2001, aged 80.

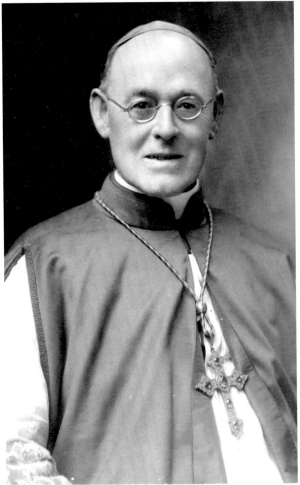

Archbishop (later Cardinal) **Hinsley** prayed for his parents at their grave during a visit to his native village of Carlton, Yorks in January 1935.

Arthur Hinsley was born on the 25th August 1865, to Thomas and Bridget (née Ryan) Hinsley. His father a carpenter and his mother was Irish. He studied at Ushaw College in Durham and the Venerable English College in Rome, and was ordained to the priesthood on the 23rd December 1893.

He taught at Ushaw College until 1897, then took up pastoral work in Westminster in 1898, serving as headmaster of St. Bede's Grammar School (which he founded in 1900) from 1899 to 1904. In 1917, after another period of pastoral work, he became a Domestic Prelate of His Holiness (14th November) and the rector of the English College in Rome, a post in which he remained until 1928.

On the 10th August 1926, he was appointed Titular Bishop of Sebastopolis in Armenia by Pope Pius XI. He received his episcopal consecration on the following 30th November from Rafael Cardinal Merry del Val, with Archbishop Giuseppe Palica and Bishop Peter Amigo serving as co-consecrators, in the chapel of the English College.

He was later named Apostolic Visitor to British Africa on the 10th December 1927.

Pope Pius XI, on the 9th January 1930, made Bishop Hinsely Titular Archbishop of Sardis and Apostolic Delegate to the British missions in Africa that were not under the jurisdiction of the apostolic delegations of Egypt, Belgian Congo, and South Africa. He retired as Apostolic Delegate due to ill health on the 25th March 1934, and was appointed a canon of St. Peter's Basilica four days later, on the 29th March.

Rather surprisingly – not least to himself – he was named the fifth Archbishop of Westminster on the 1st April 1935.

In his capacity of cardinal, Hinsely served as one of the electors in the 1939 papal conclave, which selected Pope Pius XII. He also condemned Hitler and other Fascist leaders during World War II.

Cardinal Hinsley, by now nearly blind and deaf, died from a heart attack in Buntingford, East Hertfordshire, on the 17th March 1943, aged 77.

He was buried at Westminster Cathedral, and Archbishop William Temple of Canterbury described him as: "a most devoted citizen of his country ... and a most kindly and warmhearted friend".

In the stilled crypt of London's Westminster Cathedral a brick-layer prepares to seal the tomb of William, Cardinal Godfrey, Archbishop of Westminster, following his Solemn Requiem in January 1963. The coffin wasn't entombed in the floor of the crypt because of the difficulty in cutting through the 10ft thick concrete foundations of the cathedral.

A view of the great crowd that attended open air Mass in the grounds of Westminster cathedral during the 1929 Emancipation Congress.

When 85 year old **Mrs. Mary O'Connell** paid a visit to Dublin in October 1930 it caused a huge stir and attracted large crowds. At the time Mrs. O'Connell was the last surviving parishioner to have witnessed personally the apparitions at Knock, Co. Mayo in 1879.

Only six weeks after the apparitions, Most Rev. Dr. John MacHale, Archbishop of Tuam, set up a Commission of Enquiry. Fifteen witnesses were examined and the Commission reported that the 'testimony' of all taken as a whole, was trustworthy and satisfactory.

Archbishop Gilmartin set up another Commission in 1936 to examine the three surviving witnesses of the apparition: Mrs. Mary O'Connell (Mary Byrne), Patrick Byrne and John Curry. All three confirmed their original statements given in 1879. Mrs. O'Connell gave evidence under oath from her death bed and at the end of her statement she added: "I am quite clear about everything I have said, and I make this statement knowing I am going before my God."

The verdict of this commission was that the evidence of the witnesses was upright and trustworthy, and concerning Mrs. O'Connell, it was reported that she left 'a most favourable impression on their minds'.

One wild theory considered – and dismissed – in great detail in 1879 was the accusation that the apparitions were the work of a prankster projecting magic lantern slides, based solely on the fact that the images appeared static, as distinct from the reported living and moving images of the Virgin Mary seen at other locations.

Mrs. O'Connell was resolute on the truth of what she had seen. She recalled how two Church commissioners took her statement in the schoolhouse and a fortnight later 20 more priests arrived, and carried out elaborate tests with magic lantern slides.

"They wanted to make out," she said, "that the pictures were like the ones we saw, but they were no more like them and no one could make them like the apparitions."

It was a rainy day in Feet Street, London, in October 1960, when the cardinal paid a visit to the offices of *The Universe*. Pictured *(from left)* are: *Universe* Editor **Christopher "Christy" Hennessy**; **Monsignor** (later archbishop) **Derek Worlock**, at that time a Westminster priest and previous Private Secretary to Cardinal Griffin; the writer, ex-editor of *The Tablet* and, at that time, *Universe* owner **Douglas Woodruff**, and **Cardinal Godfrey**.

Ambassadors of the Powers gather to exchange pleasantries outside Westminster Cathedral in July 1930, after the Te Deum to celebrate centenary of Belgium's independence.

This remarkable original photograph, which was found filed away in *The Universe* archives under "music and musicians miscellaneous", shows the great English composer **Sir Edward Elgar**. It was taken on the 23rd May 1931 at Kingsway Hall, London, where Elgar was about to record his Nursery Suite in the presence of the Duke and Duchess of York (later King George VI and Queen Elizabeth) – it was dedicated to their children, the Princesses Elizabeth (the present Queen) and Margaret Rose, the dedication coming from Elgar in his capacity as Master of the King's Musick.

The man with him is his record producer Lawrance Collingwood (1887-1982) whose particular claim to fame regarding Elgar came in early 1934 when the composer, a dying man, took part in a recording session of his music by means of a GPO landline linking

his home in Worcester to London's Abbey Road studios, which Elgar had opened in November 1931. Collingwood conducted and Elgar was able to comment on the performances. The man with a moustache visible next to Collingwood's left hand is W H Reed, leader of the London Symphony Orchestra and a great friend of Elgar's.

As a Catholic coda to this story, the opening movement of the Nursery Suite ("Aubade") features Elgar's hymntune Drakes Broughton ("Hear thy children, gentle Jesus") composed by Elgar at the age of 19 and revisited in his mid-seventies for this piece. The hymntune is heard on woodwind partway through the Aubade and heard again towards the end of the movement on full orchestra – impressive!

WELLS, MIRACLES AND CURES

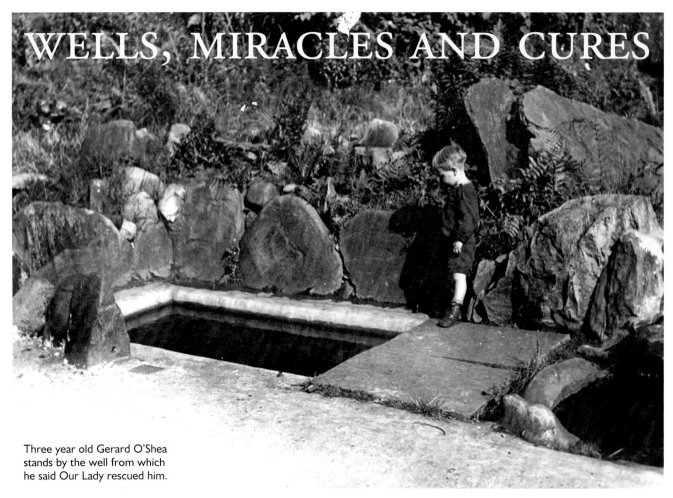

Three year old Gerard O'Shea stands by the well from which he said Our Lady rescued him.

The Shrine

Almost a century ago, a small group of immigrant Irish workers lived in a harsh industrial landscape in South Wales where two rivers met, both dirty and black with the coal washed down from the huge workings upstream.

Very much in the minority, and with the nearest church some distance away, the Catholics of Abercynon, Mountain Ash, decided to build their own parish church.

In the 1920s employment was fragile at best, so there was plenty of spare labour around to help with the project.

The site chosen for the church was a steep slope above one of the rivers and, as they cleared the land, two springs shot up just above the level of the polluted river, delivering pure, clean water.

Inspired by the event, the parish priest, Fr. Carroll-Baillie, instructed his parishioners to buuild "The Welsh Lourdes", to hold the spring water, and he arranged for a large statue of Our Lady to be purchased, and placed overlooking the grotto.

Stations of the Cross were moulded in concrete and set up along the path for prayer and meditation.

The grotto attracted many pilgrims, and there were alleged cures for skin diseases and physical disabilities.

Pilgrims travelled by the coachload from all over South Wales, and there were regular processions carrying the Blessed Sacrament from the church to the wells, with young girls scattering flowers as they went.

Today the statue of Our Lady still looks over Abercynon, but the site of the wells is in need of restoration, as are the Stations.

Despite this, many pilgrims still do find their way down the overgrown hillside to pray at this very special shrine.

The Miracle

On the 16th September 1932, *The Universe* correspondent in Cardiff filed a remarkable and touching story concerning the well at Abercynon.

A note to the editor accompanying the story reads: "An intimate friend in whom I can place complete confidence related the story to me".

The correspondent relates how one Gerald O'Shea, a three-year-old boy living at the church cottage at Abercynon, knocked at the cottage door one morning. When his mother opened it she found him to be dripping with water.

"Gerald", exclaimed his mother, "where have you been?"

Gerald answered: "I fell into the well."

"Which well?"

"The big well."

In 1932 Abercynon was a spring filliing two small pools and supplying the well in which the sick bathed at the grotto. It was to this well that the boy was referring.

When Gerald had been dried, his mother questioned him further. She was puzzled to know how the boy had got out of the well which was over three feet deep.

To her astonishment, Gerald said: "Our Lady helped me out."

He then showed his mother how Our Lady gave him her hand and helped him out. Our Lady, he said, told him to go home at once.

The child was quite calm. He showed no sign of fright nor shock at his sudden immersion in the ice-cold water.

Feeling the situation beyond her, Gerald's mother took him to the parish priest, Fr. Carroll-Baillie. Again the boy related quite simply what had happened, and described the lady he'd seen as "the lady of the medal", dressed in blue.

The Universe correspondent's "friend", after calling on Fr. Carroll-Baillie, went to the boy's home and invited him to go for a walk. Hand in hand they strolled to the grotto, where this conversation took place:

"Tell me, Gerald, where were you playing when you fell in the well?"

Gerald pointed to the place.

"How did you get out?"

"Our Lady pulled me out."

"Which lady?"

"The lady of my medal."

"Show me the medal, Gerald."

The boy unbuttoned his little shirt to show a medal which he had been wearing practically since his birth.

"Give it to me, Gerald."

"No!" (very emphatically).

The enquirer then pointed to a statue of Our Lady of Lourdes above the well and asked: "Was that the lady that pulled you out?"

"No, no, the lady of my medal pulled me out - the lady in blue."

"Gerald," asked the visitor, "would the lady pull me out if I fell in?"

"No," said the boy, "because you haven't got a medal."

Miss Marion Russell of Georges Road, Liverpool, said that a miraculous cure had been performed upon her after she immersed herself in the waters at St. Winifrede's Well, Holywell, Flintshire, North Wales. She told *The Universe* that she had "a useless arm" that had to be strapped to her side and had caused her several years of severe pain. After her visit to the well she regained the full use of it, as can be seen in this picture of her leaving home carrying her shopping bags. The picture is dated 1963, but the sub-editor's handwriting on the back is more consistent with the period 1925-1935. Any precise information would be welcome.

Eileen Lynn, aged 35, of Sandford Estate, Bramley, Leeds, had been blind and semi-paralysed for two years. Just a few hours before returning from the first post-war pilgrimage from Yorkshire to Lourdes, in September 1948, she told friends that she had recovered her sight and speech, and had regained the use of her left arm, which had been paralysed after a fall. Her sight returned suddenly, she said, during Mass in the Grotto. Eileen is pictured with her beloved budgerigar, Paddy.

Mr. William Glynn, of Ardwick, Manchester *(marked No.1)* was taken to Lourdes on a stretcher with the 1929 Salford pilgrimage, and returned able to walk without the aid of sticks. **Miss Agnes Fairbrother** *(no.2)* was also a stretcher case and had been bedridden for two years. She suffered also from loss of speech and returned able to walk and talk. The pair are pictured being greeted by the Bishop of Salford, **Thomas Henshaw**.

Archbishop Mathew, Bishop Ordinary to the Forces, is transferred by jackstay at sea from HMS Tyne, depot ship, to HMS Crossbow, destroyer, while on passage to Gibraltar in October 1954, where the Home Fleet was assembled during its Autumn cruise.
The archbishop was in Gibralter for a fortnight, visiting Catholic officers and men of the three services, after which he travelled to Malta.

The Universe reported that pupils and old boys of Beaumont College "did sterling work" as brancardiers at Lourdes during the October 1927 Catholic Association Pilgrimage, which was led by the Bishop of Northampton, **Bishop Dudley Charles Cary-Elwes**. Pictured are: (back row from left) J. Tolhurst, J. Drummond, M. Hougalt, J. Strange, H. Noule, M. Cresswell, R. Wessel, T. Hilliman, D. Drummond, H. Strange, C. Hilleman, A. Romane, W. Jones. (Front row from left) G. Hood, Capt. Harrison, Capt. P.C. Leggetter MC (who was in charge of the party), Bishop of Northampton, Brig. Gen. G.H. Harrsion CB CMG, H. Houret, G. O'Connor.

A proud day for Mr. and Mrs. Patrick Connole and their 13 children after the christening of the latest addition to the family – five day old twins – at St. Mary Magdalene's, Maltby, Yorks in July 1969. **Bishop Moverley**, Auxiliary in Leeds, went to Maltby to officiate.

Mr. Richard Everard Augustine Elwes, Q.C., O.B.E., D.L., pictured in January 1958 with his family outside Buckingham Palace, where he arrived to be sworn in by the Lord Chancellor as a High Court Judge.

Mr. Justice Elwes, as Mr. Richard Elwes Q.C., had been recorder of Northampton. He was the fifth son of the singer Gervase Elwes, who achieved particular fame as "Gerontius" in Cardinal Newman's and Elgar's "The Dream of Gerontius".

Also with Mr. Justice Elwes is his wife Mary Freya Elwes who, as

Polly Elwes (*inset*), became a well-known BBC television commentator. She was an in-vision announcer from 1957 to 1960, and reporter for the BBC's 'Tonight' programme from 1959 to 1962. She was also a regular panellist on "What's My Line?", and 'Face The Music', and contributed to the 1960s BBC Children's TV's series 'What's New?'. She is also said to have produced a London stage play in aid of the Ealing Abbey Building Fund.

She married sports broadcaster and presenter Peter Dimmock, and died on the 15th July 1987.

Church leaders in LIverpool headed a mass march through the streets of the city in March 1979 to show their solidarity with 2,400 workers of the Tyre Division at Dunlop's Speke factory, who were threatened with redundancy. "We are glad to be able to march with these men," said **Archbishop Derek Worlock**.

Although most of the glass negatives belonging to *The Universe* were thrown away in the 1980s, when the company moved to Manchester, leaving only the prints, one or two glass plates have been found. Most were of minor events, but this one revealed a remarkable scene when scanned and reversed. Deep in thought, the great Cardinal Newman sits engrossed in paperwork.

The artist **Graham Sutherland** (1903-980) poses on a ladder in February 1963 beside his latest work, a Crucifixion, above the altar of St. Aidan's Catholic Church in London's East Acton. Despite having converted to Catholicism some 35 years previously, the painting, a towering 16ft x 12ft, was his first Catholic commission. He was born in Streatham, London, attending a preparatory school in Sutton, Surrey. He was then educated at Epsom College, Surrey and Goldsmiths College, University of London. For a while he worked as an engineer at the Midland Railway Works at Derby before studying engraving at Goldsmiths College, University of London, which led him to paint full-time. Regarded in the 1940s and 50s as Britain's most important painter, his masterpieces have languished in storage for many years, including more than 600 currently in Cardiff, and a selection are displayed in the newly-built Pembrokeshire Landscape Gallery in St. David's, Pembrokeshire.

In October 1930 *The Universe* celebrated 70 years of continuous publication with a number of special events, including a banquet at Stationer's Hall, London at which the great tenor John McCormack sang. On the 5th December the staff *(pictured above)* received very welcome Apostolic Blessing from Cardinal Pacelli, who was later to become Pope Pius XII.

Priests and public cheer as they receive a blessing from Cardinal Bourne, who came on to the balcony of Archbishop's House, Westminster in June 1934, as part of the celebrations of the golden jubilee of his ordination to the priesthood.

Cardinal MacRory, Archbishop of Armagh and Primate of All Ireland, pictured at Downside Abbey in July 1937, where he gave his blessing to a group of nuns among 6,000 pilgrims who'd gathered to honour Blessed Oliver Plunket, Armagh's martyr-archbishop, who had been executed at Tyburn in 1661.

An uncompromising display in the Catholic Workers' Bookshop, opened by the Franciscan Fathers in Peckham in 1938.

A break for prayer along the route of the annual Lowestoft – Walsingham walk in August 1969.

Every week during 1942 *The Universe* printed a paragraph announcing that the Southwark Travelling Mission would at the weekend visit one or other of the many Mass centres that had recently been established in churchless districts of the diocese, and that Mass would be celebrated at some barn, stable, inn or house. In November of that year **Father P. Donnelly** went to Paddock Wood, and is seen here celebrating Mass in the annexe of the Kings Arms.

Monsignor Bruce Kent *(in white t-shirt)* comes to the end of his 500 mile sponsored walk for a nuclear-free world at the gates of the Royal Ordnance factory in Burghfield, Berks, on Hiroshima day, August 1986. He then moved on to the main gate of the Atomic Weapons Research Establishment, Aldermaston *(pictured above)* to plant a number of radiation hazard signs.

Born on the 22nd June 1929, Bruce Kent was for many years probably Britain's best-known peace campaigner and member of the Campaign for Nuclear Disarmament (CND). He served as General Secretary from 1980 to 1985, and as Chair from 1987 to 1990. He was born in London in 1929 and was educated in Canada before attending Stonyhurst College, and then St. Edmund's College, Ware. He served as an officer in the Royal Tank Regiment from 1947 to 1949 and afterwards read Jurisprudence at Brasenose College, Oxford from 1949-1952.

In 1958 he was ordained as a Catholic priest and acted as Catholic chaplain to the University of London from 1966 to 1974. He was Chair of the charity War on Want from 1974 to 1976. In 1987, he retired from active ministry rather than comply with an instruction from the late Cardinal Basil Hume to desist from involvement in that year's UK General Election.

In 1992 he was a candidate for the Labour Party in the constituency of Oxford West and Abingdon – sitting MP and former Conservative minister John Patten retained his seat.

He remains a regular writer on Catholic affairs, and is Vice-President, CND, Pax Christi and the Movement for the Abolition of War.

Bishop Cormac Murphy-O'Connor with his dog Daniel joins young people at the beginning of a 20 kilometre sponsored walk through the Sussex countryside in October 1984.

Actor **Patrick McGoohan** enjoys a joke with his wife, the actress Joan Drummond, whilst they were being interviewed for *The Universe* in the late 1960s.

McGoohan was born in Astoria, Queens, New York City to Thomas McGoohan and Rose Fitzpatrick, who were living in the United States after emigrating from Ireland to look for work.

Shortly after he was born, McGoohan's parents moved back to Mullaghmore, Dromahair, County Leitrim, Ireland and, seven years later, they moved to Sheffield.

With the outbreak of the Second World War, McGoohan was evacuated to Loughborough, Leicestershire, where he attended Ratcliffe College, excelling in mathematics and boxing.

McGoohan graduated from college aged 16 and returned to Sheffield where he worked variously as a chicken farmer, a bank clerk and a lorry driver before getting a job as a stage manager at Sheffield Repertory Theatre.

When one of the actors became ill, Patrick filled in, launching his acting career. He fell for an actress named Joan Drummond, the woman to whom he reportedly still writes love notes every day. They are still considered one of show business's happiest couples. They were married between a rehearsal of *The Taming of the Shrew* and an evening performance on 19th May 1951. They have three daughters, Catherine (b. 1952), Anne (b. 1959) and Frances (b. 1960).

On a few occasions McGoohan has played the part of a priest. In 1955, McGoohan starred in a West End

production of a play called *Serious Charge*, in the role of a priest accused of being gay. Orson Welles was so impressed by McGoohan's stage presence in the production that he cast him as Starbuck in his York theatre production of *Moby Dick Rehearsed*.

While working as a stand-in during actress screen tests, McGoohan was signed to a contract with the Rank Organisation between 1930 and 1960, the producers casting him as the conniving bad boy in such films as the gritty *Hell Drivers* and the steamy potboiler *The Gypsy and the Gentleman*. After a few films and clashes with the management the contract was dissolved.

Free of the contract, he did some TV

work and continued on the stage, and soon producer Lew Grade approached him about another contract, this time for a TV series, the spy show *Danger Man*.

McGoohan said 'yes' but with a few stipulatons: all the fistfights should be different, the character would always use his brain before using a gun, and, much to the horror of the executives, no kissing. They hired him anyway.

During the fourth season of filming, McGoohan told Lew Grade he was going to quit. Grade asked if he would at least work on "something" for him, and McGoohan gave him a run-down of what would be a mini-series about a secret agent who resigns suddenly and wakes up to find himself in a prison disguised as a holiday resort.

Grade asked for a budget, McGoohan had one ready, and they made a deal over a handshake early on a Saturday morning to produce *The Prisoner*.

McGoohan has appeared in many films, including *Ice Station Zebra*, for which he was critically acclaimed, and *Silver Streak*, with Gene Wilder and Richard Pryor.

He is most recognised today by a new generation of fans as the Machiavellian King Edward "Longshanks" *(pictured left)* from the 1995 Oscar-winning *Braveheart*.

After retirement, McGoohan lived in Los Angeles with his wife of 57 years. As well as his three daughters, he had five grandchildren. On the 11th June 2008, he became a great-grandfather to Jack Patrick Lockhart.

McGoohan died on the 13th January 2009.at Saint John's Health Center in Santa Monica, California, following a brief illness.

The children of St. Mary's school choir, Ponders End, Middlesex, were entralled by the dark, sonorous bass voice of stage and television star **Frank Olegario**, when he visited the school in December 1970 to take part in a choral concert run by the Knights of St. Columba to help parish funds. Frank has played numerous film and TV roles, perhaps most famously he was "merchant no:1" *(inset)* in *Indiana Jones and the Temple of Doom* (1984). He was also "man in a Fez" in the 1971 James Bond film *Diamonds are Forever,* and he played alongside Kenneth More and Lauren Bacall in the part of Rajah in the 1959 film *North West Frontier*.

Dr. John C. Heenan, Archbishop-Elect of Westminster, wearing his purple robes, is pictured seated in a car on his arrival at Euston Station, on 18th September 1963, having travelled down after saying farewell to his flock in Liverpool. It's a little-known fact that the archbishop nearly didn't make it, after the train he was travelling in had to make an emergency stop at Stafford, after an anonymous caller told police that a bomb was on board! All 450 passenger were evacuated from the train while a search was carried out. Nothing was found. Dr. Heenan later commented: "I was not in the least concerned. It would have been very inconvenient if a bomb had gone off."

A note on the photographs:

In the interests of historical accuracy we would like to point out that the information given in this publication derives from newspaper cuttings and written captions attached to the original photographs. Whilst every effort has been made to ensure the accuracy of this information, we cannot be responsible for any inaccuracies that may have existed in the original text. If you are aware of any such errors, or can supply additional information about the photographs, we would very much like to hear from you at the address below.

Although some the photographs are marked with exact dates, it is clear that in many instances these represented either the date that the picture was catalogued for publication, or the actual publication date, and not necessarily the precise day on which the event took place. Under the circumstances we have restricted the date to the year and month given, unless it has possible to confirm the exact day.

We would like to thank the photographers who gave permission for their images to be reproduced. We would also be happy to hear from those who we were unable to locate.

From The Archives of the Universe Catholic weekly
produced in collaboration with *The Universe* Catholic weekly
4th Floor, Landmark House, Station Road, Cheadle Hulme, Cheshire SK8 7JH.
Tel: 0161 488 1700   email: joseph.kelly@totalcatholic.com

Editor: Joseph Kelly